AF577094

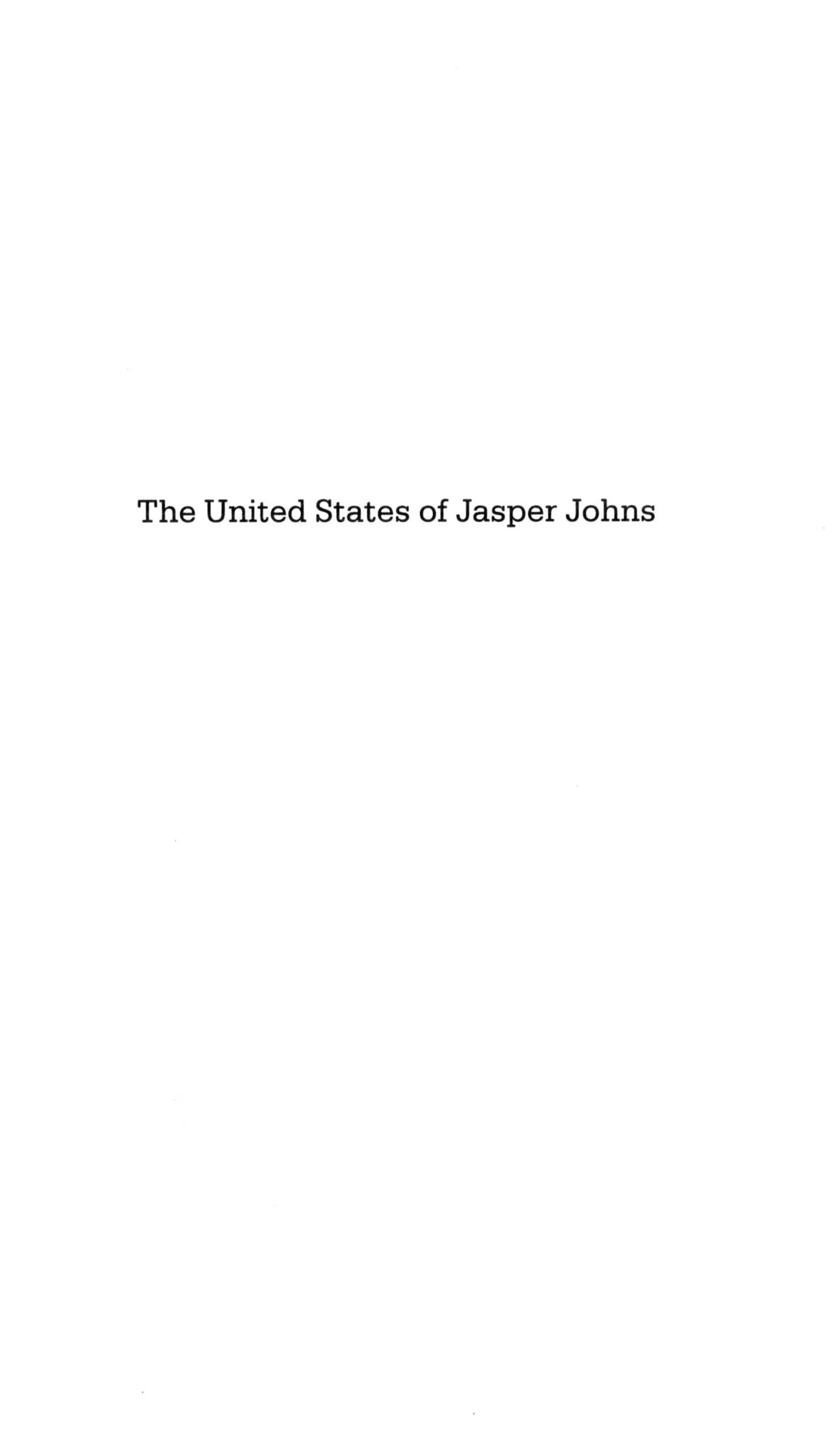

The United States of Jasper Johns

John Yau

The United States of Jasper Johns

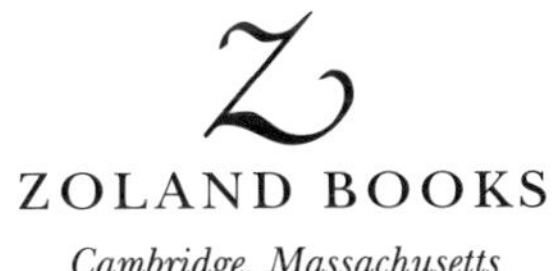

ZOLAND BOOKS
Cambridge, Massachusetts

First edition published in 1996 by
Zoland Books, Inc.
384 Huron Avenue
Cambridge, Massachusetts 02138

FIRST EDITION

Book design by Glenn Suokko
Printed in the United States of America

03 02 01 00 99 98 97 96   8 7 6 5 4 3 2 1

This book is printed on acid-free paper, and its binding materials have been chosen for strength and durability.

Library of Congress Cataloging-in-Publication Data

Yau, John, 1950–
The United States of Jasper Johns / John Yau. — 1st ed.
p. cm.
ISBN 0-944072-75-5 (alk. paper)
1. Johns, Jasper, 1930– —Criticism and interpretation.
2. United States in art. I. Title.
ND237.J66Y38 1996
759.13—dc21   96-47265
CIP

Acknowledgments

Neither a piece of writing nor a work of art is made in complete isolation. For all the time the writer or artist spends alone, numerous individuals contribute in one way or another to that person's undertaking. This book is no exception. I wrote it with the help of editors, poets, and painters. I would like to thank Ted Berrigan (1934–1983), Clark Coolidge, Russell Ferguson, David Frankel, Stephen Frankel, Phil Freshman, Bill Jensen, Margrit Lewczuk, Terry Myers, Archie Rand, David Reed, Dorothea Rockburne, Raphael Rubinstein, David Shapiro, Nick Wilder (1938–1989), and Trevor Winkfield for their comments and observations.

A big, warm thanks to Leo Castelli for his early commitment to this book.

Many thanks to both Agnes Gund and Sally Ganz for inviting me into their homes.

Thanks to Ingrid Sischy for commissioning me to write

about Jasper Johns for *Artforum,* to Susan Lorence and Bob Monk for commissioning me to write on *Lead Reliefs,* to Elizabeth Armstrong for asking me for an early version of this essay for *Jasper Johns: Printed Symbols* (Minneapolis: Walker Art Center, 1990), and to Paul Schimmel and Donna De Salvo for asking me to contribute an essay to *Hand-Painted Pop: American Art in Transition 1955–1962* (Los Angeles: Museum of Contemporary Art, Los Angeles, 1993). These opportunities encouraged me to rethink what I had previously written.

Thanks to Sandy Martiny, Julia Haywood, and Suzanne McClelland for all their research.

I would like to thank Sarah Taggart, Jasper Johns's assistant, who for more than a decade has been incredibly gracious and timely in providing me with materials that were essential to the writing of this book.

I would like to single out and thank Eve Aschheim for her honesty, faith, and acuity, all of which I needed to finish this book.

Finally, I would like to thank Jasper Johns for the many hours we have spent together during the past fifteen years, and for the many pleasures I derived from discovering in our conversations what can and cannot be said about poetry and art.

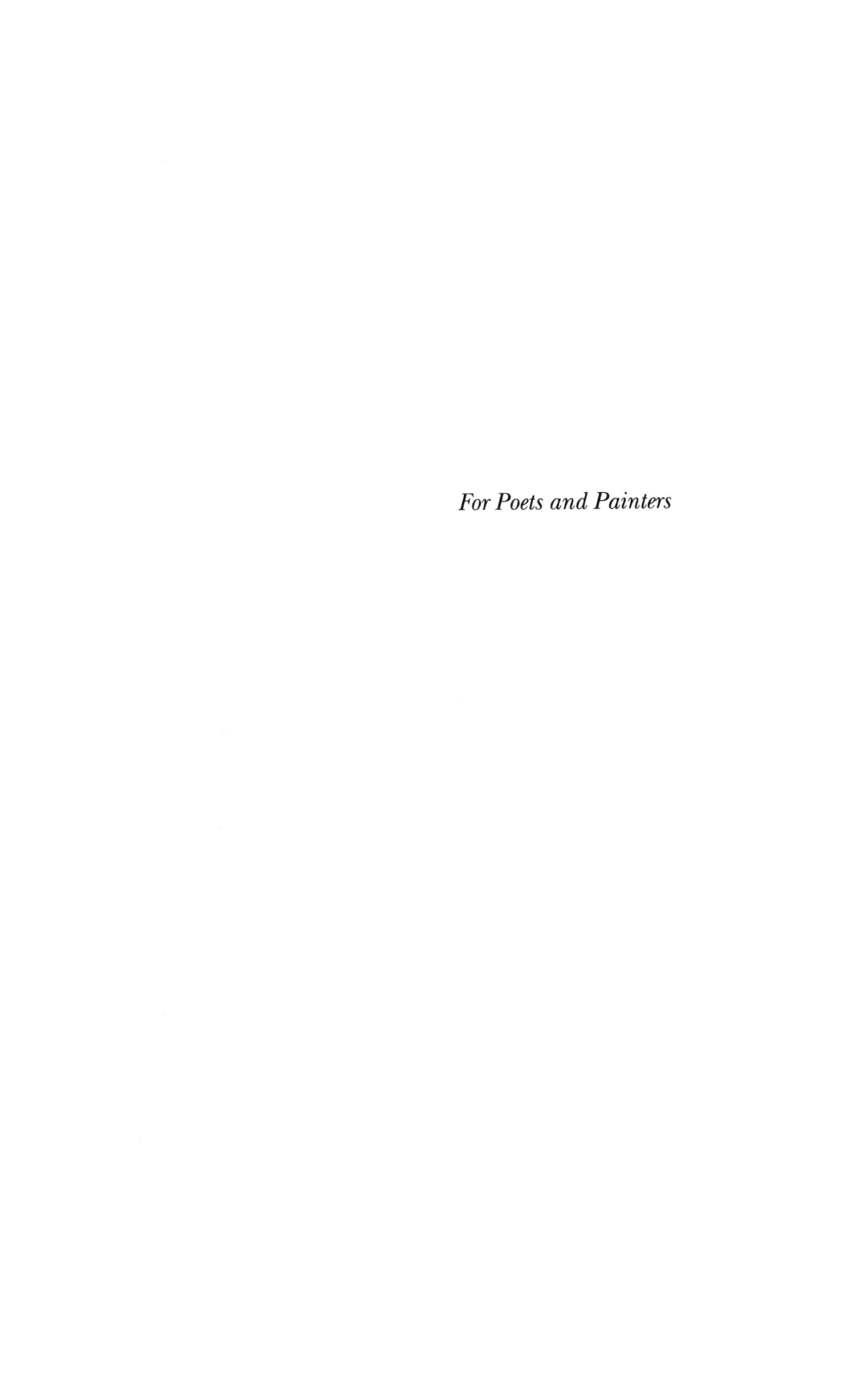

For Poets and Painters

I'm interested in things which suggest the world rather than suggest the personality. I'm interested in things which are, rather than in judgments.

Jasper Johns

Contents

One

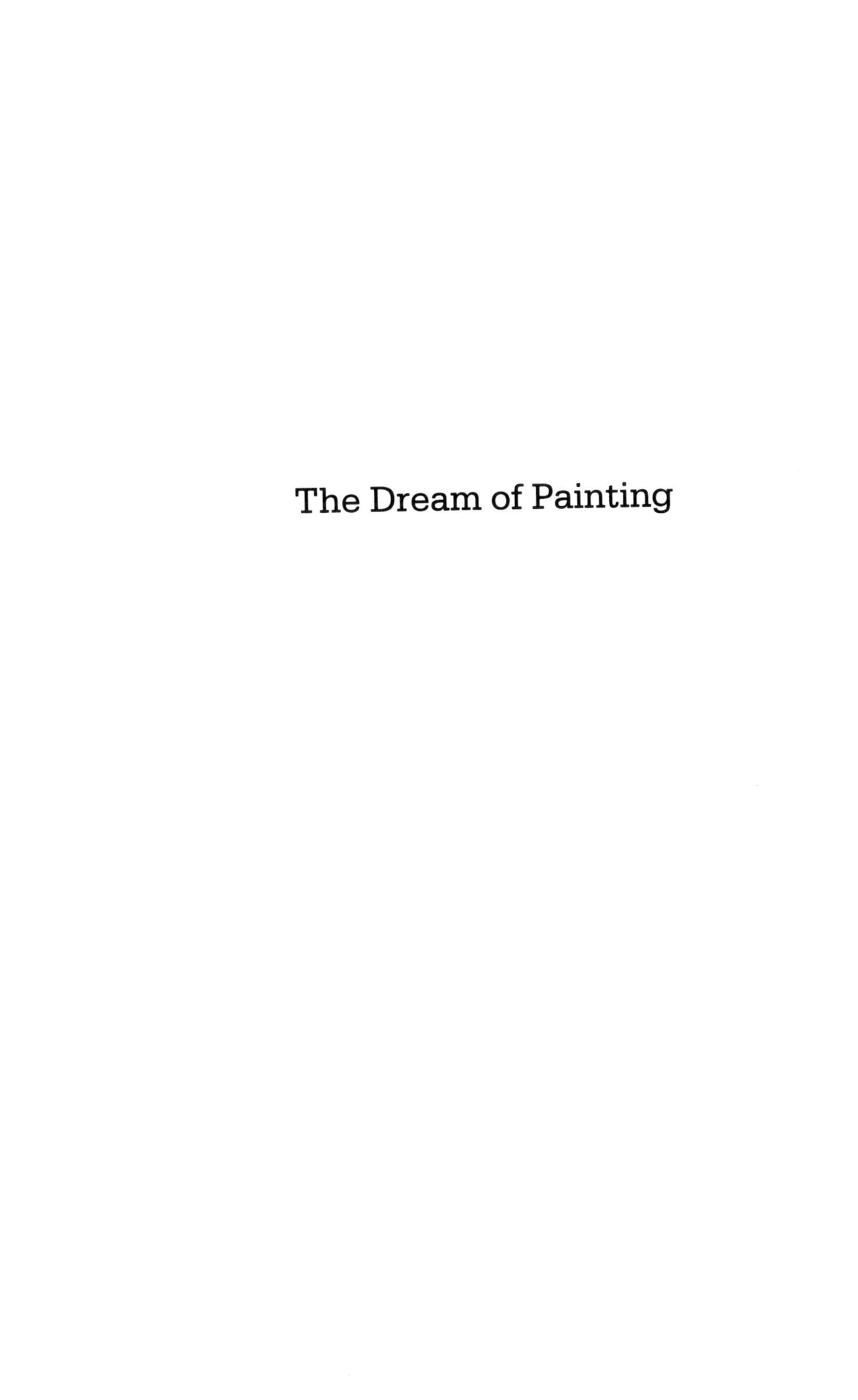

The Dream of Painting

The desire for immediacy is overwhelming, and this desire is perhaps more strongly felt in painting than in writing, which must always deal with what is absent. One of the issues painters must face is how to locate this desire in a medium which cannot overcome its own physical presence; they must grapple with what that presence could mean in a secular world where no belief or ideology is central. For while painting is no longer a way to show the viewer that the earthly world is connected to the heavens, so we can believe that we will be released from what we are and become what we dream, the desire for presence remains unabated. But if the goal of painting is to recuperate what lies beneath all appearances, to come in contact with what is real beneath the myriad of social realities in which we exist, how can one be a painter whose yearning for knowledge isn't satisfied by evoking the unmediated, insisting on the literal, or believing in metaphor? After all, these modes of expression are rooted in tradition, and thus at bottom are more social than recuperative.

How does a painter make the actual of art coincide with the actual world? This question has haunted artists from Sassetta and Giotto to the present. Of all the artists working right now, Jasper Johns is the one who manages to penetrate the realm of appearances until he glimpses what the individual is in the world, its ravaging continuum.

Johns has wrestled most fully with the central problem of painting: how to use the medium to construct a process of perception which enables the artist to be in touch with the real, how not only to recuperate the real but also to make that domain accessible to the viewer. This is very different from making a painting of objects or making a painting into an object or surface to be perceived. Although this might not be immediately apparent, Johns does neither.

Johns's art is predicated on his awareness that all of living is directed toward the moment when one's mind and body are joined together as lifeless matter, which is of course the very stuff of which painting is made. However, rather than express disgust with painting's inability to overcome mortality, or make gestures as if such boundaries don't exist, Johns uses art to examine both the unpredictability and the limitations of experience and knowledge. His work always engages the elusive relationship between experience and knowledge, which is a substantially different enterprise than exploring the relationship between art and reality, as if they are fixed realms. Johns utilizes art to ask: How can painting and sculpture, which are embodiments of lifeless matter, reconcile the individual to his or her fate?

Although nearly a decade separates the paintings *Flag* (1955, encaustic, oil, and collage on fabric mounted on plywood [three panels], 41 1/4 x 60 3/4 in., Museum of Modern Art, New York) and *Map* (1963, encaustic and collage on canvas, 60 x 93 in., collection Agnes Gund), it will become apparent that the seeds for *Map* were planted in *Flag*. This proposition isn't surprising until one considers the possibility that the connection between these works goes deeper than Johns's incorporation of flat representational objects (a flag and a map) into the realm of painting. Johns has discovered a more profound connection between the symbol of a nation and a pictorial representation of both its geographic and its social boundaries. It wasn't simply the flatness of a flag and map or the fact that they were about America that attracted his attention. Had this been the case, Johns would have been nothing more than an artist who used irony to pander to an art world audience that was both jaded and alienated.

The connection between the flag and the map goes to the heart of Johns's work, which is his recognition not only that the individual lives in a world of uninterrupted change but that society, which is the collective expression of individuals, repeatedly denies this fact. If reality, which is to say the world we inhabit, is continually reformulating itself, then how does one both recognize and accept a process which eventually subsumes us all? How can the individual be true to change and entropy, which is the stuff of life, rather than uphold the social ideals of stasis and its concomitant illusion that any one of us can exist outside time and chaos, which is the stuff of much art?

One of the distinguishing characteristics of Johns's intense awareness of time passing is his ability to manifest his perception through reconstructions of representational things which both embody stasis while also proving that time does not stand still. He shows us how he perceives an object most of us take for granted; he recontextualizes its existence in reality. In doing so Johns calls many of our presumptions about reality, both as flux and as social construct, into question. If time doesn't stand still, what does it mean to use a flag and a map, two social representations that don't register the passage of time, as ways to examine the individual's relationship to change? It is Johns's pointed questioning, and the way he frames his inquiry, calling attention to the deep-seated deceptions inherent in familiar symbols, ordinary objects, and common representations, that makes his work urgent, necessary, and, ultimately, profound.

Johns has said on a number of occasions that he started *Flag* because of a dream in which he saw himself painting the American flag. This suggests that he simply responded to the dream. However, it was not the object but the dreaming of it which engaged him. For Johns making a painting of an American flag was not the issue. That would have meant he tacitly subscribed to the Newtonian ideal of cause and effect, that one simply reacts to certain events. Instead, Johns wanted to make a painting which reconstructed the meaning of the dream.

On a technical level, *Flag* is neither a painting nor a sculpture. Rather, it disrupts the traditions of painting and sculpture by integrating a layered image and a pictorial object into a single work. And while many observers consider it a hybrid work, which combines features attributed to both painting and sculpture, it is more accurate to describe *Flag* as Johns's reconstruction of something he has seen as well as his revelations about it; he transforms his perceptions of the world he inhabits into something both physically and visually palpable. Johns directly engages both our senses (touch and sight) and our intelligence (reading and memory) with what he places before us. By addressing both the viewer's animal senses and reasoning intelligence, he underscores his interest in the shifting relationship between the body and the mind, and how this relationship shapes one's perceptions of flux.

Flag focuses on the continuum between memory and perception. In it Johns is trying to actualize the moment when looking supersedes memory and an engagement with reality can begin. The very familiarity of *Flag's* design reinforces the likelihood that memory and habit prevent us from looking at the world, that these faculties enable us to avoid being actively engaged with and by reality. For often when we think we have seen this "thing" or "place" before, we no longer actually look at it, no longer enter into a dialogue with its existence.

Instead of dismissing a dream, as many of us have often done, Johns located a "flag," which is a symbol of utopian commonness, in the gap between remembering something we have seen many times and seeing something anew, seeing something about it we have not previously noticed. Typically, a flag is a symbol that helps citizens believe they stand outside time and change. It sums up a moment of resolution in a collective history, as if that moment is neither mythically narrative nor subject to disruption or revision. Like most flags the American flag represents both a belief in unity of purpose and the existence of a common social reality. It is a palpable symbol which proposes that the world will go on being the same, and that its existence within the world as a meaningful object is guaranteed.

In *Flag* Johns reveals not only these and other fallacies inherent in the American flag but also the facts that what all of us share is inescapable seclusion and what makes us individuals is that the daily nature of this isolation is unique. The dream reinforced Johns's sense of both reality's sequestering effects and the uniqueness of its power; he had had an experience that others hadn't. At the same time Johns used pieces of newspaper and cloth dipped in hot wax to reveal the persistent fantasy many viewers continue to invest in painting, which is that time can be frozen into permanent presence, and that the resulting aesthetic experience is proof that all of us inhabit a secure world. The dream's disruptive power clarified for Johns that both real flags and paintings, whether traditional or modernist, embody the beliefs that the individual can transcend his or her isolation, that chaos can be endlessly deferred, and that transformation will occur in an orderly fashion.

If we subscribe to the comforting power society associates with a flag and a painting, are we not enlisting them in our desire to believe that isolation and dissolution aren't inevitable, even natural conditions? In this regard society has endowed both the flag and art as sanctuaries from reality. Since the beginning of his career, Johns has denied himself the inherent misconception of this option. He knows art can neither protect him from life nor offer him lasting solace. Rather, one of the deepest reasons Johns makes art is to register with clinical accuracy one's existence in the continuum of time passing. Because Johns makes art which is in tune with his progress in real time, he avoids the pitfalls of solipsism, which haunt contemporary art that isn't overtly social, as well as resists the pressure to make art which is timely.

Johns has often said that the flag inspired him to pick the target, map, numerals, and alphabet as subject matter, because they are "things seen and not looked at, not examined." He has also said about them: "They were preformed, conventional, depersonalized, factual, exterior elements."[1] What is it about the factual element of an American flag that we have seen but not examined? After all, as many observers have pointed out, a flag is a flat thing and in this regard is similar to a painting. But this observation is largely aesthetic, and, as I have already suggested, I believe Johns's interest in the flag goes deeper.

By inserting a "flag" into the site usually reserved for painting, Johns underscores the deepest deceptions a flag and a painting share. It is only by revealing these deceptions that he can clarify his insights into the individual's relationship to reality. For while a flag and a painting share certain physical properties, such as being pieces of cloth which have been colored in a particular way, they are also things which both a nation and an individual use to defer their awareness of existence as an isolating process of continual and often painful change. Flags and paintings both embody and point to the existence of an ideal world; this is the lie they have in common.

One can say that beliefs remarkably similar to those associated with a flag are also an inherent part of the long tradition to which paintings (and art) belong. Certainly in most Christian art, which is the basis of Western art, both the artist and the viewer presumed that art was proof of their unabiding faith in an afterlife. But in a secular world, where such beliefs can no longer be guaranteed, what can painting show us? This is the question Johns began answering in *Flag*.

We know that nothing goes on being the same, that change occurs at all sorts of speeds, that one experiences only part of everything that occurs in daily life, and that transformation and randomness are the deepest, isolating facts of our lives. Yet knowing these things doesn't mean we embrace them or even measure our lives by them, certainly not to the extent that I believe Johns does. By breaking down the barrier between an American flag and a painting, as well as by using various materials to construct a "flag" in the place of painting, Johns overturns the hierarchy separating art from life. Neither, he repeatedly shows us, is more important than the other, because neither can escape time. And if we give art a privileged position in our daily life, which is the position it had during the age of religious belief, then we are saying that art offers us a respite from life and from chaos.

Flag vividly demonstrates that art, if it is to be true to life, cannot ignore reality and change. For as each of Johns's "flag" paintings, no matter how similarly they are made or look, is unique, so is each American flag. Johns's "flags" are only superficially alike. A row of equal-size American flags may look exactly alike, but each of them inhabits a unique and separate reality, which in turn is part of a larger, more inclusive reality. This is the deepest fact that the individual and a flag have in common; whether flesh or cloth, each is essentially cut off from all others made of the same material.

One of the shifts that has occurred in Johns's work over the past forty-plus years is that he has grown more acutely aware of time passing. Paintings such as *Racing Thoughts* (1983, encaustic and collage on canvas, 48 $^{1}/_{8}$ x 75 $^{1}/_{8}$ in., Whitney Museum of American Art), and *After Holbein* (1993, encaustic on canvas, 32 $^{9}/_{16}$ x 25 $^{5}/_{8}$ in., collection the artist) are suffused with his attempts to give both visual evidence and physical substance to the process of inevitability, to what the future holds for us all. He wants to look openly at time passing and embrace the insights this looking offers even as he passes from it. One could say that Johns's homely items are indistinguishable from his perception of them. They only seem to typify a flag, a map, or a blueprint of a two-story house which has been taped to a wall; they are not in any way "realist" nor do they attempt to fool us into thinking they are real. Johns's interest in transforming these objects into art goes deeper than aesthetics.

Flag is like a flag and not like a flag; this paradox initiates our scrutiny. We want to see what makes the painting like a flag, our first impression, and what makes it different. And when we begin really looking at the painting, examining it closely, we cross the threshold separating memory from experience. *Flag* stirs us to enter the state of looking and examining in an attempt to become intimate with the world we inhabit, more conscious of the way we routinely ignore or accept it.

On its deepest level, *Flag* owes its existence to the Greek philosopher Heraclitus, who observed: You cannot step in the same river twice. However, to be continually conscious of the fact that one is caught in time often leads to a deep and inescapable sorrow, even bitterness. Time is merciless; it ravages us all. Johns's paintings may seem to hint at this unrelievable sorrow, but they never succumb to it. His refusal to point to himself as a victim of time, thus privileging his experience over that of others, is the result of tact and understanding; we are all victims of time, all essentially isolated from others by its unfolding. This is what we have in common. Thus, for all the expressiveness we feel emanating from his work, Johns is not an expressionist, not someone who believes in the usefulness of distortion or exaggeration.

In reenacting a dream, and in being true to its reality, Johns had to ask: What does it mean to remember a dream? One answer is that the dreamer is examining a reality which exists only in his mind. A dream is the opposite of the collective experience symbolized by the flag. It is a reality which shows the dreamer how separate and isolated he is from others. Thus, in undertaking the painting Johns had to look at the flag anew and discover whether its reality could reveal to him something about his isolation.

The dreamer also asks: What and where is one's body in a dream? Dreams take place in the mind, but they seem to involve the entire body. Johns saw himself painting a flag, which is to say he saw his body doing something and later remembered doing it; the separation between mind and body becomes more apparent when one is remembering a dream. For at the moment of dreaming, when the reality of the dream is so intense that it will be remembered the following morning when one is awake, what is the relationship between one's mind and body? Do we remember what happened in a dream or do we remember what we think happened? Are the flowers we smell in a dream real flowers? Or do we dream that we are smelling flowers which are not really there? And if they are not really there, what is the relationship between a dream and reality? Is one more real and thus more important than the other? What is the act we have committed in a dream when there is no evidence of it. Which self has had the dream, the waking self or the dreaming self? What is the relationship between these selves when, as all of us know, the dreaming self is quite capable of committing acts the waking self would never consider? It is in Johns's perceptual analysis of his dream that the meaning of *Flag* resides.

For Johns, *Flag* is palpable visual evidence, but of what? That he had a dream, because he has told us so and because he has made a painting which reinforces his story. If we believe this answer, then the painting becomes either autobiographical and anecdotal or hermetic and inaccessible, neither of which is true. However, if we believe *Flag* is neither anecdotal nor hermetic, then we must try to discover what evidence Johns wished to reconstruct while making it and whether what he realized about his dream was profound. The question we should ask here is whether the significance of *Flag* is primarily aesthetic. Is the importance of *Flag* and other early paintings by Johns the result of the immense and immediate influence they had on his peers, and the sea change they initiated in the history of art? Or does *Flag's* importance lie in its meanings and the way it generates them?

If we believe the significance of *Flag* and Johns's work in general is purely aesthetic, then we accept the likelihood that art can only be about art, that the yearning for both immediacy and knowledge can only be expressed in aesthetic terms. In this case reality remains inaccessible, and the empirical world forever eludes us. However, if we believe that the significance of *Flag* is the result of the meanings contained in its construction, then we are inclined to believe that art can address questions beyond the realm of aesthetics. I believe that the questions Johns asks unveil the nature of reality, that they have enabled him to come in contact with how forsaken and transformed human beings are by time's passing. It is this need that informs all his work, no matter how calmly realized it appears in the end.

By now we know that Johns's approach to *Flag* led him to discover encaustic, a material he would quickly make central to his art, and that he didn't know what the outcome of the painting would be, only that it should closely resemble an American flag circa 1954. He used a bedsheet, which he cut into three different-size rectangles, each corresponding to one section of the flag. He planned to complete each section and then join them.

The three sections consist of one which corresponds to the flag's canton, its blue square with white stars, another which corresponds to the seven stripes (four red and three white) in the section adjacent to the blue field, and the third, whose counterpart is the six stripes (three red and three white) running the entire length of the flag. By separating the bedsheet into these sections, Johns both more effectively focused on the problems raised by the juxtaposition of one area with another and alluded to the splits one experiences when remembering a dream.

A bedsheet evokes the site of dreams. Johns chose this item because it was the largest piece of blank cloth at hand, which suggests the urgency with which he approached the subject. Until his dream Johns had for the most part made small box-like objects, and he didn't have a large piece of canvas in his studio. While working on *Flag* he switched from enamel to encaustic because he got tired of waiting for the oil to dry; he also found it difficult to keep both the white stars and their surrounding blue field and the alternating red and white stripes distinct from each other. Having learned about encaustic in a book he found in the bookstore he worked in for a short time, and having experimented with it in a small sculptural object, *Star* (1954, oil, beeswax, and housepaint on newspaper, canvas, and wood with tinted glass, nails, and fabric tape, 22 5/8 x 19 3/4 x 1 7/8 in., The Menil Collection, Houston), which he made for a friend, Johns realized that this material possesses certain properties which could help him resolve the compositional problems posed by the design of the American flag.

Encaustic is made of beeswax. It usually comes in a solid form, which the artist must heat. Once it is liquid, the artist can mix pigment into the viscous medium, thus making the desired color. In contrast to enamel, encaustic begins to harden the minute it is removed from heat. Because it hardens rather than dries, the artist can apply it in discrete layers, as well as in isolated areas. After the encaustic has been applied to a surface, it must be heated again; this seals the painting. In this last step, the temperature must be just right or the wax will begin melting. Finally, encaustic is a preservative which seals other materials, such as paper collage, protecting them against the effects of time.

In *Flag*, Johns used encaustic in an unconventional manner, which became an essential part of his early methodology. He dipped bits of newspaper and cloth in the appropriately colored encaustic and applied them to a surface he had already covered with pieces of newspaper and other printed matter. Before dipping these fragments he cut or tore them so that, like puzzle pieces, they defined, as well as corresponded to, the appropriate borders. Where the wax dripped beyond the demarcated boundaries, Johns later applied another layer of the appropriately colored wax. Some of the edges of the collage elements are more flush with the stripes' boundaries than others, and the pieces have been lined up in rows. Johns wasn't painting a "flag" but constructing an object, and in this regard *Flag* is similar to *Star* and other early works. He was not yet a painter, but, through rather unconventional means, he was making a painting.

Since he didn't abandon this painting and start another one, the bedsheet becomes more significant, at least in the artist's mind. He didn't get rid of the site where the dream might have taken place, which would have been the sensible thing to do since the combination of wet enamel, newspaper, and encaustic is potentially a conservator's nightmare. Moreover, at some point, the painting was damaged and had to be reworked, so the dating of the newspaper collage isn't consistent.* Finally, a few years after it was completed, *Flag* was mounted on plywood. When I mentioned the instability of this combination of materials to Johns, and the difficulty of preserving the painting, he replied, "Yes, it's falling apart, just like me."[2]

At the same time Johns's commitment to the original painting suggests a deep reluctance to abandon something once it is started. He wants to see things through, to learn if they can bring him in touch with the actual while preserving the record of the changes in the painting. Although most of the printed material in *Flag* seems

---

* According to Johns, he had hung *Flag* on a temporary wall, which was accidentally knocked over during a party given jointly with Robert Rauschenberg, who lived in the same building. Among the people attending the party were Morton Feldman and Philip Guston.

to have been used without regard to the words or images it contains, in one instance Johns made a choice, which was most likely the result of serendipity. Placed in the middle of the composition, and visible only if one stands close to the painting, is the phrase "Pipe Dream." Because it is both prominently located and correctly aligned, whereas many of the other collage pieces are on their sides, the phrase can be read as evidence of Johns's admiration for the Belgian Surrealist painter René Magritte, whose work he and his friend the artist Robert Rauschenberg saw at the Sidney Janis Gallery, New York, in March 1954, shortly before Johns had his dream.

Titled *Magritte: Word vs. Image,* this large exhibition contained a wide range of Magritte's paintings which combine words and images, many being shown for the first time.[3] Among these paintings were Magritte's first word painting, *La Clef des songes* (*The Interpretation of Dreams,* 1927, oil on canvas, 38 x 55 cm, Staatsgalerie Moderner Kunst, Theo-Wormland Sammlung, Munich) and the first version of *La Trahison des images* (*The Treachery of Images,* 1929, oil on canvas, 60 x 81 cm, Los Angeles County Museum of Art), in which the artist placed a precisely painted image of a pipe above the phrase "Ceci n'est pas une pipe" (This is not a pipe). Certainly a number of the other paintings in the exhibition, among them *Les Reflets du temps* (*Reflection of Time,* 1928, oil on canvas, 54 x 73 cm, private collection, Belgium), *Le Masque vide* (*The Empty Mask,* 1928, oil on canvas, 73 x 93 cm, Kunstsammlung Nordrhein-Westfalen, Düsseldorf), and two paintings with the same title, *Le Sens propre* (*The Literal Meaning),* both 1929 and one of which Rauschenberg bought in the early 1960s, can be said to anticipate work by Johns.*

Johns's deep admiration for Magritte has led him to collect a number of the artist's works, the most significant being *La Clef des songes* (*The Interpretation of Dreams*), 1935, which is one of a handful of paintings in which the artist

---

* Magritte's depiction of a clock and the words *ciel* ("sky") and *canon* ("gun" or "a rule or law") in *Les Reflets du temp* can be seen as a precursor to a number of "Untitled" paintings Johns did in the mid-1980s depicting a wristwatch "pinned" to the middle of an enigmatic face in which the eyes and mouth (mountain) are flush with the edges.

In *Le Masque vide,* Magritte's depiction of the backs of four canvases, on each of which has been written a word or phrase, shares something with *Canvas,* 1956, in which Johns has attached the front of a covered wooden stretcher to a larger canvas surface and then covered all of it with gray encaustic.

In one of the paintings titled *Le Sens propre,* Magritte depicted two oddly shaped framed surfaces, each containing a word, leaning against a wood-paneled wall, thus anticipating the trompe l'oeil wood paneling Johns first depicted in *Perilous Night,* 1982. The stone wall Magritte depicted in the other painting titled *Le Sens propre* is clearly the stylistic precursor of the flagstones which first appeared in Johns's *Harlem Light,* 1967. Certainly the number of affinities between the paintings in the Janis exhibition and Johns's subsequent work at radically different phases of his career suggests something more than coincidence.

juxtaposed images with English words.[4] In the painting Johns owns, Magritte divided the composition into four compartments. In each he juxtaposed a word and an image. Thus, the top left compartment pairs the image of a horse's head with "the door." The top right compartment pairs a clock with "the wind." The bottom left compartment pairs the image of a white porcelain water pitcher with "the bird," and in the bottom right hand compartment, rather uncharacteristically, Magritte paired the image of a suitcase with "the valise," which in both French and English designates the same thing. Johns bought this painting, which is stylistically similar to the *La Clef des songes,* 1929, that he saw in 1954, in the early 1960s, a few years after his work started gaining attention.

Magritte's word and image pairings were inspired by the format of reading primers,[5] anticipating Johns's use of the American flag, map, alphabet, numerals, and ruler, all of which a child repeatedly encounters in elementary school. At the same time, reading primers utilize silhouettes and outlines, which both Magritte and Johns would incorporate into their lexicons. Magritte, however, was interested in word association and the range of speculation that exists in the gap between words and things, whereas Johns, in early paintings such as *False Start* (1959, oil on canvas, 67 1/4 x 54 in., private collection), reveals the incommensurability between words and what they are supposed to signify. For Johns language is not consensual; we have not completely agreed upon what words mean or how they are to be used. This lack of agreement extends to the artist's "flags" and "maps," while his "alphabets" and "numerals" are both silhouettes and letters signifying only themselves. Thus, the act of naming inspired Magritte to poetic theorizing about the nature of reality, but for Johns the act of naming is riddled with frustration. The words (or letters) point only to themselves. If one attempts to deduce an autobiographical aspect to Johns's early work, one sees that, beginning at a young and impressionable age, he regarded "flags" and "maps," symbols a society uses to socialize its children, as lies.

Another difference between Magritte and Johns is that the former transformed images pictorially, depicting an object (a table) in a material other than that in which it usually occurs (stone), whereas Johns uses materials such as encaustic and bronze to transform an object (a flag or a coffee can crammed with paintbrushes) materially into its double, thus preserving its essential features. Johns probably derived the aspect of naming from Magritte, and he did so at a time when Surrealism was scorned by most artists and critics.

While Johns's collage fragment acknowledges the influence of Magritte, it also comments on an affinity shared by an American flag and a painting; both are "Pipe Dreams." Johns's collage also documents that the source of the painting was a dream that he had had, as well as embodies his own doubts about his ability to complete a painting which was badly conceived and likely to remain unfinished; it was still a "pipe dream." As *Flag* was the first time Johns affixed printed material dipped in wax to the surface, he must have been unsure about its outcome.

Initially, Johns may have been interested primarily in encaustic's propensity to harden quickly in discrete areas. As he learned about the medium's properties, he began recognizing that its idiosyncrasies echo the inherent reality that nature repeats itself even as the individual is inexorably pulled forward in time, toward dissolution and chaos. Encaustic is always susceptible to extremes of heat and cold, and can be made to melt or crack. Consequently, unlike oil paint, which exists more or less in a static state once it is used, encaustic exists in a cyclical continuum that stretches from solid matter (or form) to liquid (or dissolution) to solid matter to potentially liquid again.

At the same time, by heating encaustic and introducing both pigment and collage into it, Johns permanently changed it. The encaustic bonds with the pigment and collage so that it cannot be made to return to its original, translucent state. Despite the continuum there is no going back; one can only move forward in time. This susceptibility of encaustic to irrevocable transformation echoes the effects of time on the individual.

In *Flag*, Johns used encaustic to bind together the design of a flag (a symbol of harmony, unity, and time stopped) and pieces of a newspaper and other printed material (evidence of temporality). A flag envisions a utopian future bordering the present, whereas a newspaper sums up the past as if it is ongoing. Yet, preserved just below the surface of the encaustic and literally within it, the pieces of precisely dated newspaper are getting older and more remote from us as we look at the painting. We can inhabit neither the future nor the past, but are caught between them.

The printed fragments alert us that *Flag* is not a flag: they are both a visual irritant and a material equivalent of memory. Glimpsing something embedded beneath the encaustic, we are compelled to move closer to the painting, to shift our attention from seeing the entire composition to closely scrutinizing different areas of the surface. In doing so we begin to see phrases such as "Pipe Dream" but lose sight of the whole painting. Such changes and shifts in attention remind us that our engagement with reality is not fixed, that our eyes are continually changing in relationship to reality, which itself is continuously changing.

In addition, we can neither take in the printed materials all at once nor actually touch them, a tension that parallels our inability either to inhabit the past or fully to comprehend our present. Thus, not only are both the future and the past remote but the present is in flux. After all, we never see *Flag* in its entirety, never take in the design and the collage simultaneously. Switching modes of comprehension, we go from looking to reading and back again. Consequently, instead of upholding the hierarchical belief that art is a privileged object capable of conveying a pure (or purifying), timeless aesthetic experience, which we receive all at once, Johns's use of encaustic to bind together printed material (both dirty artifacts connected to a past moment and something to be read) and a "flag" (a false vision of a collective moment in history and something to be seen) loosens painting from its aesthetic confines, makes it occupy the contingent world we all inhabit.

Johns has suggested that his project was determined by a handful of questions: "I had the wish to determine what I was. I had the feeling that I could do anything.... But if I could do anything I wanted to do, then what I wanted to do was find out what I did that other people didn't, what I was that other people weren't.... It was not a matter of joining a group effort, but of isolating myself from any group. I wanted to know what was helpless in my behavior—how I could behave out of necessity."[6]

It is striking that Johns repeatedly uses the word *what* rather than the expected *who.* This choice underscores his concern with delving beneath the bedrock of appearances, with recuperating the actual. Had Johns been more interested in defining his artistic identity, he could have attempted to restate what the older generation of Abstract Expressionists had accomplished, subjective expression, objective statements, or art about art. However, neither the unified self (or expressive "I") nor pure art (selfless, objective statements) interested him. Instead, he focused on a dream, which is both a manifestation of helpless behavior and evidence of a divided "I."

Johns recognizes that one's knowledge of reality is at best fragmented, impure, and incomplete. He may incorporate attributes associated with the traditions of abstract art, still life, portraiture, and trompe l'oeil realism, but in the final analysis his art belongs to none of these traditions because he refuses to subscribe to the ideologies and belief systems inherent in each of them. Here we should recognize that his work's resistance to broad categories such as painting and sculpture as well as its rejection of more narrow categories such as realism and trompe l'oeil representation are marks of his originality.

Johns knows that time's effects on the individual's material existence are essentially isolating. This is what his dream made clear to him. In *Flag* and other paintings done between 1954 and the winter of 1958, the year of his first solo exhibition at the Leo Castelli Gallery, New York, Johns chose a course which eschewed both subjectivity and objectivity, particularly as these modes were defined by the Abstract Expressionists. If realizing the nature of his material body is what Johns is after, which I believe it is, then the viewer is compelled to ask: How does *Flag* retain Johns's perceptual process? How is it both evidence of what is "helpless" in his behavior, and proof that he or any individual is isolated from all others?

On the level of appearance, *Flag* closely resembles an American flag; its blue rectangle contains forty-eight stars, and there are thirteen alternating stripes, seven red and six white. Even after we've seen *Flag* many times, what still initially strikes us is the similarity between the painting and an American flag. But what also strikes us, almost at the same time, is the difference between the painting and a flag.* Both the uneven surface and the visibility of readable material help differentiate the painting from its real-life counterpart. There is an unsystematic roughness to the painting which is elemental in its power. The

* The same year Johns completed *Flag*, he did a pencil drawing, *Flag* (1955), which has sixty-four stars.

layered surface is not the result of expressiveness but an inherent aspect of the combination of materials. At the same time, the painting is simultaneously visual and physical, the combination of encaustic and collage privileges neither image nor physicality, looking nor reading.

The matter-of-fact brushstrokes are physical and semitransparent. However bound together they are by the overriding design, each star and stripe both defines and inhabits a distinctly separate domain. As in an aggregation of silhouettes, each marks out the isolating conditions of its individuality. *Flag* is not merely the image of a flag but an object that has been cobbled together. The stars hover between individuality and being part of a larger pattern; despite their similarity each one is different enough to be distinct. As in a mosaic, the stars are segregated but contingent. Each was made by dipping a piece or pieces of material into hot wax and then setting it in place.

Whereas earlier representations of stars in paintings, such as the pattern of gold stars on the frescoed ceiling of Giotto's Arena Chapel (Padua), are proof of a society's belief in reconciliation and immortality, and the belief that the resurrected individual will be embraced by nature itself, Johns's stars and stripes are embodiments of solitariness. For him the stars may be part of nature, but they are proof of neither reconciliation nor resurrection.

Flag not only wrenches the stars from the symbolizing impulses of Western art, but calls the very basis of that tradition into question.

Typically, a silhouette is a flat, monochromatic image which defines both the limitations of its existence and its isolation from the world, an isolation that is material rather than introspective. Thus, while the flag's canton is derived from a cultural tradition that stretches at least as far back as Giotto,* Johns understood his dream to mean that the flag was a palpable silhouette made up of palpable silhouettes. Rather than being a symbol of humankind's harmonic relation with nature, and the various manifestations of unity and integration such beliefs imply, it defines a state of extreme isolation, internal divisions, and the disruptive power of time over the individual. In this regard the flag echoes the act of dreaming, which was proof of what was "helpless" in Johns's behavior. For not only did the dream separate him from all others but the flag could be understood as expressing the realizations that each of us dreams and that our dreams ultimately seclude us from others. When Johns reconstructed this process of perception in *Flag*, he revealed

---

* The tradition of artists involved with the creation of sacred spaces is very much a part of Modernism. Picasso, Matisse, Rothko, and, more recently, Brice Marden, James Brown, and Archie Rand have all made work with specific sacred spaces in mind.

the false premises upon which a real flag is based.

In *Flag,* Johns has constructed a continuum that begins with the smallest element, the silhouette of a star, which he sustains throughout the painting. No matter how unified by design and composition, every element of the painting occupies its own reality. Although dipped in encaustic, the pieces of printed matter don't lose their identity. At the same time the hardened brushstrokes are visible. Thus, the isolations and divisions are not just on the picture surface; through layering they penetrate the work.

Although it is easy to overlook the words "Pipe Dream," and they are not visible in reproduction, Johns has also included another phrase in the painting. Made of individual white letters which peek through the blue field, the words "United States" are visible in the lower left-hand corner of the flag's canton; they are the linguistic counterpart of the west coast of the United States (a section of a map) which Johns dipped in encaustic and placed in the lower left-hand corner of the red stripe running along the bottom of the flag.

Johns abbreviates the full title "The United States of America" to simply "United States," thus recontextualizing it in light of his dream.* With its three panels and silhou-

---

* The "U" of "United" is rotated so that one first reads "nited States," a pun which both evokes the dream and anticipates the painting *Perilous Night* (1982) and its pun (Night=knight).

ettes, *Flag* unites the states of waking and sleeping by acknowledging their contiguousness, as well as their isolation. In contrast to Magritte's pairing of word and image, Johns's pairing of "United States" with a "flag" results in the words being the actual thing they describe. Like the canton full of stars, the phrase is made of separate, palpable identities. Johns's reduction of the phrase "The United States of America" to "United States," and his placement of them within the composition, are deliberate acts requiring much attention. However, I believe that he never intended the words to be so easily overlooked, that he introduced them into the composition out of his desire to be truthful to the union of separate states actualized by remembering a dream.* In subsequent "flag" paintings, he no longer felt it imperative to include these words because their source was *Flag*, not a dream.

The stars, each representing one state in the union, are both a "United States" and a "Pipe Dream"; they embody a vision of unity and agreement that Johns finds false.

---

* The words are not visible in any of the reproductions I have examined, which suggests one reason why they have been overlooked. The falseness of the reproductions reinforces Johns's commitment to reality. We can only come in contact with the meaning of the painting through primary experience. The irony is that artists such as Andy Warhol and Frank Stella, both of whom Johns influenced, made art which did not lose its meaning in reproduction. Thus society once again reifies the realm of appearances.

In his painting it is their distinctiveness and solitariness that gain our attention. A flag may offer individuals some sort of refuge, but it cannot provide solace from either the metamorphosis induced by time or the extreme solitude that such states of awareness underscore. The individual may believe he is part of something "united," but in actuality the individual occupies a separate and distinct state and in turn is made up of separate and distinct states, the five senses and the mind.

Johns wasn't satisfied with feeling he could paint anything; for him the ideal of artistic freedom was an illusion, as false in its premises as the solace offered by the flag. He wanted to connect his mind to his body, to understand what was "helpless" in his behavior, and thus to come to terms with those parts of his being over which he had no control, his body and his "racing thoughts." The dream clarified Johns's isolation from others as well as underscored the individuality of his perceptions, which are the basis of his thinking and being. While the individuality of our perceptions is common to us all, much of our living is a denial of this condition, which society both encourages and makes possible. However, the individual is at best a "united states" of the five senses and the intelligence, the body and mind.

It is Johns's burden repeatedly to acknowledge this realm of perceptual awareness and the recognition that one is permanently secluded from others as well as riddled by deep irreconcilable divisions. The unified self or "I," which Sigmund Freud was one of the first to expose as false, and which Ludwig Wittgenstein further called into question when he revealed language's woeful deficiencies, is really multiple and fragmented. The dream of the integrated self seems more and more an ideal which one can try to approach but never fully arrive at.

At the same time, the shifting relationship between the senses and the intelligence makes the apprehension of reality problematic, even when one repeatedly refuses, as Johns does, to succumb to the desire for asylum. While not everything in *Flag* is immediately visible, the painting doesn't hide its meanings. It is apparent, for example, that the painting is made of three sections which have been joined together, thus defining a condition of both unity and separateness. From the moment he cut the bedsheet, Johns knew he was initiating an investigation into a condition present in himself and us all. The questions raised by his dream would plague him in his subsequent work.

The rather ordinary map of the United States that Johns alludes to in *Map* (1963) is a diagrammatic conjunction of nature and culture; it demarcates and names states as well as fixes the shifting boundaries of natural phenomena such as the Pacific Ocean and the Gulf of Mexico. This conjunction of nature and culture, which he first explored in *Flag*, constitutes Johns's subject; it is what many of the objects he has chosen have in common. His ale can, for example, evokes the cycle of consumption and waste, while the rim of a bathtub reminds the viewer of the link between cleanliness and dirt, order and entropy. Johns's vocabulary consists largely of objects derived from the world; they are both self-contained and contingent.

In *Map*, Johns used a stencil to give the states and various bodies of water their assigned names, but he did not take a systematic approach. For instance, he stenciled ATLANT in black letters over a violet-colored ATLANTIC. The last two letters of the black word have been cut off by the painting's edge; this suggests that no representation of reality is all-inclusive and also conveys reality's shifting states. Among other things ATLANT alludes to the lost continent of Atlantis, a place considered both fictional and real. Johns's unsystematic approach is also apparent in his decision to use abbreviations in some cases (N.D.), whereas in others he spelled out the entire name (South Dakota). This approach further extends to the use of color, largely muted tonalities of gray punctuated by few bright primaries. The result is a low-key visual cacophony; our attention jumps and shifts from the names to the irregularly shaped rectangles designating specific states and back again. In this regard our perception of the painting mirrors its existence; we are a "united states" of seeing and reading.

In the area designated ATLANT, and just above the abraded word, Johns vertically aligned three irregularly edged rectangles (red, yellow, and blue), their right sides flush with the painting's edge. Because they are in primary colors, and thus largely out of tune with the rest of the painting, the three rectangles seem to function as a key which (like the separate states) name only themselves. Above the primary rectangles, its top edge flush with the painting's right edge, Johns has collaged a fragment of a newspaper: "New York Post, Friday, October," locating the painting in time and space.

As with the newspaper collage in *Flag*, this and other pieces of collage can only be discerned when the viewer stands extremely close to the painting and is no longer able to see the entire composition. Again the edges of some of the collage elements are flush with the states' boundaries, but others are not. Embedded beneath the painting and thus covered by the encaustic, the collage fragments are evidence of temporality; they reinforce the painting as a collision between being a record of time's passage and the frozen "present" inherent in every kind of pictorial representation.

Johns knew that the function of a flag and a map is to reify order and stasis in the face of time's unfolding, to repudiate reality. In order to loosen them from their fictional status, he had to revive their potentiality for being authentic. One way he achieved this goal was by underscoring the silhouettes inherent in each. *Flag* names, visualizes, and embodies a state of deep and permanent isolation and irreconcilable splits, while *Map* names, visualizes, and embodies a state of continual perilousness in which the separate states cannot be integrated even if the encaustic is broken or melted. Rather, the separate states mirror the discreteness of encaustic, while the brushstrokes in the Atlantic and Pacific areas mirror encaustic's potentiality to become liquid. Yet because he has made a flag and a map subjects, Johns must be seen as a recuperative artist who is interested in the physical world.

Faith and faithlessness are not the issue. Johns is concerned with the materiality of one's existence rather than the spiritual possibilities various forms of faith might bring; the only Hell he recognizes is dissolution, the moment when the body and mind are consumed by time. He made an equation between dissolution and time's power quite clear in *Map*. In the right-hand corner, directly below ATLANT and the primary rectangles, and forming a loosely aligned vertical row that extends down from the "New York Post" collage fragment, he stencilled JOHNS, 1963 (the year the painting was completed) and the word HELL in a line. Echoing the primary rectangles, Johns drew three sides of a rectangle (the left side is open) around the line formed by the stenciled signature, date, and HELL. Where the viewer expects to see the rectangle's fourth side, the artist made a series of slanting vertical strokes in grayish encaustic. These strokes not only extend from the open, drawn rectangle to the primary rectangles but also cover the J of JOHNS, leaving the viewer to read: OHNS 63 HELL.

While the proximity of the artist's name and HELL tempts the viewer to think this is a personal, expressive statement, such an interpretation would isolate these words from the rest of the painting and deny the pairing between name and place that occurs throughout. Johns not only paired ATLANT and ATLANTIC with the correct area, but also paired them with HELL. What binds all the names to this area is encaustic (like water), susceptible to both heat and cold. Hell is dissolution; it is becoming liquid and thus losing the shape of one's body. At the same time, dissolution is a constant feature of daily life, which is evoked by the collage fragment of the newspaper. By layering the names (ATLANT and ATLANTIC) with place and the encaustic brushstrokes, Johns connected the painting to layered and shifting reality.

At the same time, the encaustic brushstrokes reinforce the shift away from the personal. Instead of JOHNS, the viewer sees OHNS and hears two puns, "one's" and "owns." This leads us to consider the likelihood that Johns wanted to convey "owns hell," "one's hell," or, combining the puns, "one's own hell." Hell is the final dissolution from which one cannot escape.

Johns echoed the "Atlantic" side of the painting by layering grayish-blue encaustic brushstrokes over the areas known as California and Arizona. It's as if the "Pacific" has washed over the western states. Not only is the integration of separate states impossible, but the process of dissolution has already taken hold. Nature, *Map* suggests, cannot be contained by the names or boundaries we apply to it.

Map is a layered, compacted structure which hovers between integration and disintegration. The "United States" neither achieves unity nor finally falls apart, though its existence is forever threatened. While this state of threat may allude to a historic event Johns witnessed, such as the Cuban Missile Crisis, it seems likely that this was not the motivating reason for making the painting. Rather, Johns recognized the illusion of order in a map and sought to reconstruct it so as to embody his perception that the individual, made up of distinct states, is constantly in flux.

The resemblance between a map, which is a neutral

and orderly diagram, and *Map*, which is agitated and layered, is largely the result of memory; the viewer recognizes that a map of the United States was the source of the painting, the subject of the artist's attention. But why a map?

One reason is that the map is a solid body surrounded by water, which echoes the relationship between the collage fragments and the encaustic. The difference is that in John's *Map*, the encaustic preserves artifacts such as pieces of newspaper, which are connected to time's passing. As a solid body surrounded by water, *Map* anticipates *Racing Thoughts* (1983), *The Bath* (1988), and *Untitled* (1988), where the subject is a body immersed in water. Time has passed: Johns is closer to the final stages of dissolution.

As with *Flag*, but spurred by the marks reformulating our memory of such a map, the viewer moves from the realm of recognition to the threshold of looking, begins registering various conditions which differentiate the painting from a typical map of the United States. Like *Flag*, *Map* is neither a metaphor nor a literal restatement but a reconstruction. Johns's effort to recuperate reality results in acknowledging time's isolating power. Since *Flag*, he has remained on a course that few artists, much less individuals, are willing to undertake. For him the only goal is to remain true to his inconsolable predicament, in the hope that some sort of pleasure might be gained from the insights he will discover.

Two

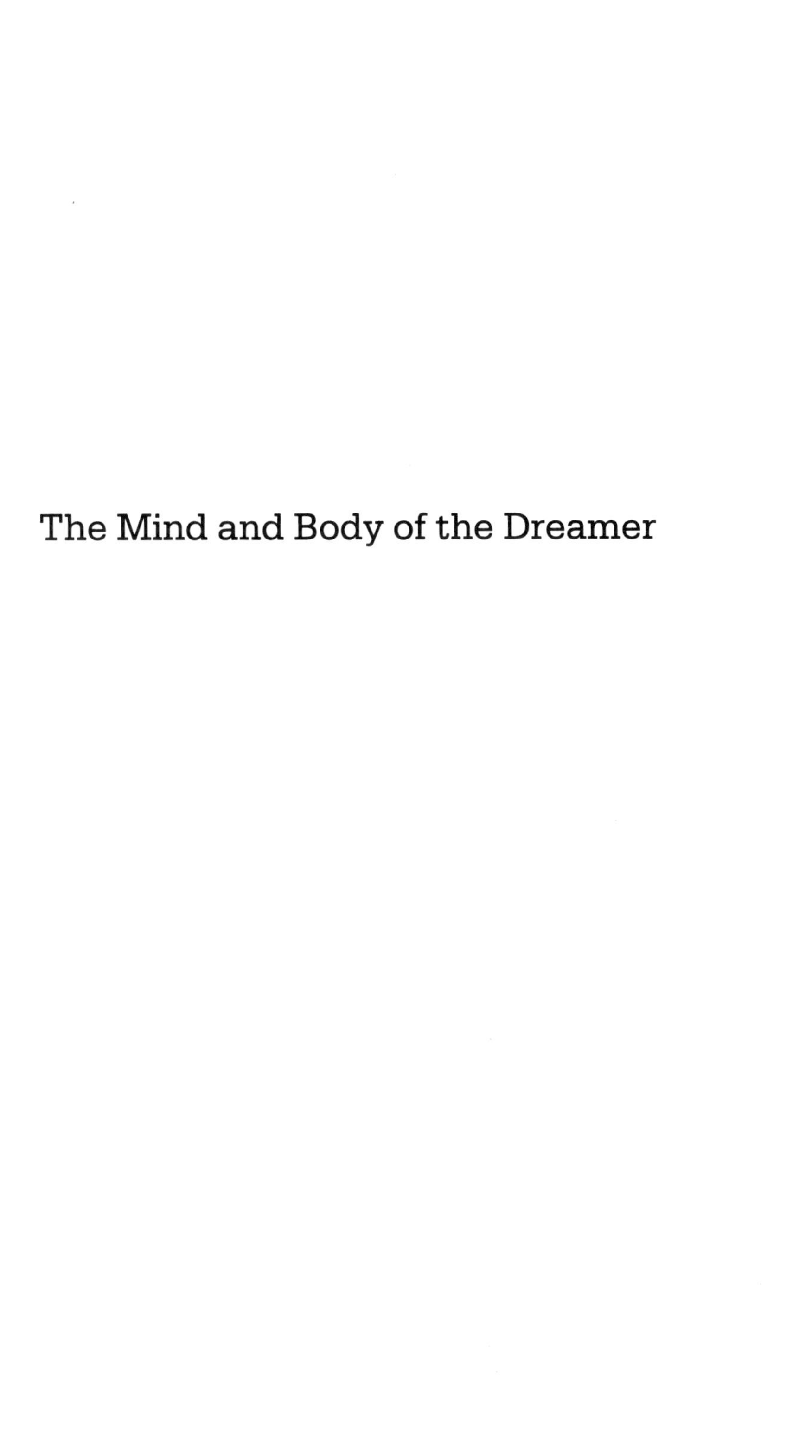

The Mind and Body of the Dreamer

In the the spring of 1965, Johns published "Sketchbook Notes"[7] in a quarterly magazine, *Art and Literature*,* of which the poet John Ashbery was an editor.** It remains Johns's most public attempt to develop a set of flexible propositions which describe not only the shifting relationship between the mind and the body, but also their relationship to the world. Because this is one of the few public statements made by an artist who has repeatedly been characterized as "hermetic," it should be read for the light it can shed on his work. Certainly someone who writes and publishes is likely to be interested in both meaning and disclosure.

Rather than seek asylum in a previously established discourse and align himself with tradition, Johns took it upon himself to develop terms—at once limited and expansive—that possess the power to name the states he felt constituted his being, the randomness of his sensations and wildness of his thinking. Such terms would help him understand something more about the ways he

---

* The first English translation of Maurice Merleau-Ponty's essay "Cézanne's Doubt" appeared in the same issue of *Art and Literature.* Work by Frank O'Hara and Ted Berrigan also appeared in this issue; Johns would allude to both poets in his work long before they became well-known.

** The editorial board consisted of John Ashbery, Ann Dunn, Rodrigo Moynihan, and Sonia Orwell.

comprehended reality, help him glimpse the order it possesses. This is very different from imposing a pre-existing order upon reality, and it is Johns's attentiveness to the world which links him to Leonardo and Cézanne, artists for whom he has professed admiration.

Johns knew that if he was truly isolated from others, and to some degree from himself, he had to construct a language that could suitably account for that isolation, make him secure within its boundaries while further connecting him to the actual. It had to be a language without blame, as calm and as obdurately matter-of-fact as *Flag*. Otherwise, his isolation would be a pose, and the real force motivating his actions would be dependence and the need for approval. At the same time, Johns knew that by articulating such terms he would be reinforcing the likely permanence of his solitude. For while the terms might help him understand his predicament, they also would stand between him and others.

Johns's terms propose something about his relationship to what Wittgenstein called a "state of affairs." Like *Flag* and *Map*, "Sketchbook Notes" is his analysis of the way he perceives his existence in the world as well as understands his changing relationship to time's unfolding. Although "Sketchbook Notes" consists of three dense paragraphs followed by a list, I want to focus on the middle paragraph, which is simultaneously poetic and theoretical, and far more narrative than either the first or the last paragraph.

> The watchman falls "into" the "trap" of looking. The "spy" is a different person. "Looking" is and is not "eating" and "being eaten." (Cézanne?—each object reflecting the other.) That is, there is a continuity of some sort among the watchman, the space, the objects. The spy must be ready to "move," must be aware of his entrances and exits. The watchman leaves his job and takes away no information. The spy must remember and must remember himself and his remembering. The spy designs himself to be overlooked. The watchman "serves" as a warning. Will the spy and watchman ever meet? In a painting named SPY, will he be present? The spy stations himself to observe the watchman. If the spy is a foreign object, why is the eye not irritated? Is he invisible? When the spy irritates, we try to remove him. "Not spying, just looking"—Watchman.

The first and last paragraphs consist mostly of ideas and methods. The writing is largely a list of materials and methodologies. Thus, the first paragraph says:

> Put a lot of paint & a wooden ball or other object on a board. Push to the other end of board. Use this in a painting. Dish with photo & color names.

Along with this kind of writing, Johns makes two observations worth noting: "encaustic (flesh?)" and "Beware of the body and the mind. Avoid a polar situation." In addition to Cézanne, he mentions Duchamp, whose own writings may have been one of the inspirations for "Sketchbook Notes." However, in the middle paragraph Johns introduces two figures which leave the reader wondering, who are the watchman and the spy? What do they have to do with Johns and his work?

The "watchman" is Johns's term for the body, while the "spy" is his term for the mind. As he has already stated, he must "avoid a polar situation." Typically, a watchman guards things which do not belong to him, and a spy is someone whose true identity remains a secret. "The watchman," Johns tells us, "falls 'into' the 'trap' of looking." That is, he becomes the article he is looking at, the flag or map. The reason this transposition occurs is because "'looking' is and is not 'eating' and 'being eaten.'" In the first paragraph Johns considered the possibility that "encaustic" is "flesh." He understood that by dipping the pieces of newspaper into encaustic, he was inducing the hot wax to both eat and not eat a foreign substance. The encaustic (or body) both consumed and preserved a foreign object. The newspaper is comprehended by the mind rather than the body. "If the spy is a foreign object," Johns wrote, "why is the eye not irritated? Is he invisible? When the spy irritates, we try to remove him."

Among other things, Johns is alluding to *Flag,* which because it must be both looked at and read, cojoins aspects of the body (watchman) and mind (spy). Thus, within the reality proposed by his terms, the combination of encaustic and collage is Johns's equivalent of the body and the mind; they are a "united states" in which each maintains its own identity. At the same time, looking is paired with eating (a form of consumption) and not eating (a form of preservation); and this dualism is paired with encaustic's ability to consume and preserve an object. In order to be true to flux, as well as to the body and mind, encaustic must consume and preserve objects which engage aspects of both looking (the body) and reading (the mind). Common to his paintings and sculptures is their engagement with these two aspects of our perceptions. Had Johns used encaustic to consume an object that disregarded either the body or the mind, he would not have avoided a "polar situation." This is why Johns has never been interested in becoming either a pure abstract artist or a conceptual artist who eschews the use of paint; he does not want to privilege body over mind or vice versa.

Underlying all the writing in this paragraph is the possibility of reciprocity, of one thing or gesture both becoming another and being preserved by it. At the same time, by linking looking and eating, Johns acknowledges that the cycle of consumption and waste is an integral part of art, which makes the enterprise impure and material rather than pure or spiritual. Johns's conjunctions also make it clear that his art arises out of an attempt to reconstruct a perceptual process, embody the moment he passed from the realm of seeing to the act of looking or what he terms "spying." Thus, when he says of Cézanne, "each object reflecting the other," he is suggesting something about his own work. The objects of his art (flag, map, bathroom wall, or blueprint) mirror his perception of them, as his materials (newspaper and encaustic) mirror each other. In the 1980s, expanding upon his understanding of Cézanne, Johns began arranging objects *(Mona Lisa* poster, faucets, highway warning sign, empty rectangle of a bathroom wall) so that they purposefully mirrored each other, manifesting his resonant perception of being caught in time.

"Sketchbook Notes" is not the first time Johns paired "looking" and "eating." *Painting Bitten by a Man* (1961, encaustic on canvas, 9 1/2 x 6 7/8 in., collection the artist) is a vertical rectangle covered with a thick layer of encaustic. In the middle of the upper third is a bite mark, where Johns sank his teeth into the painting.* By pre-

---

* In a conversation with the author, Johns revealed that he found it

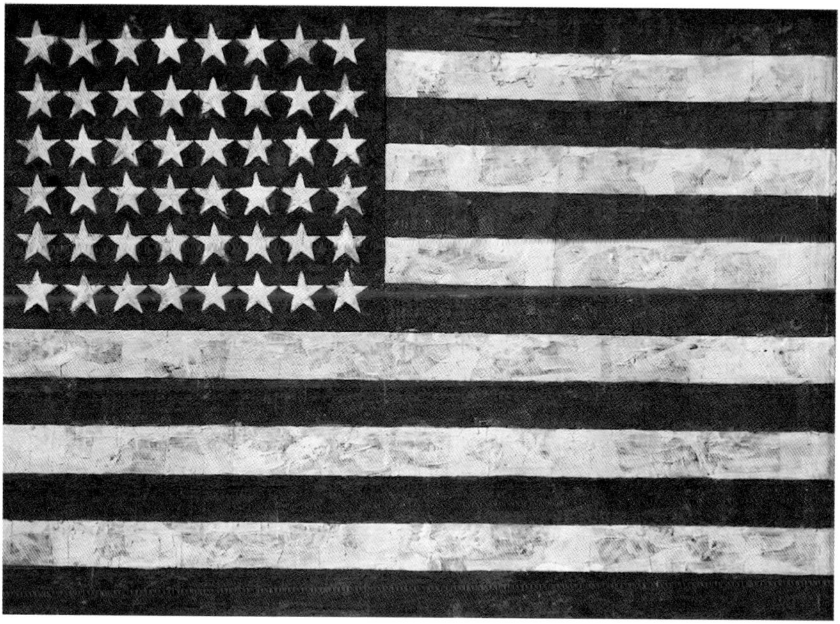

Flag, 1955, encaustic and collage on canvas, 41 1/4 x 60 3/4 in.

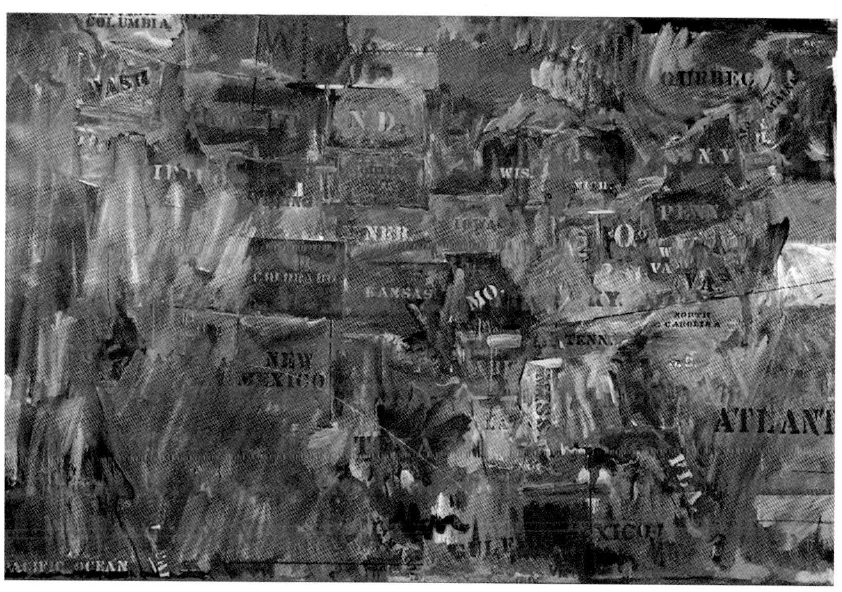

Map, 1963, encaustic and collage on canvas, 60 x 93 in.

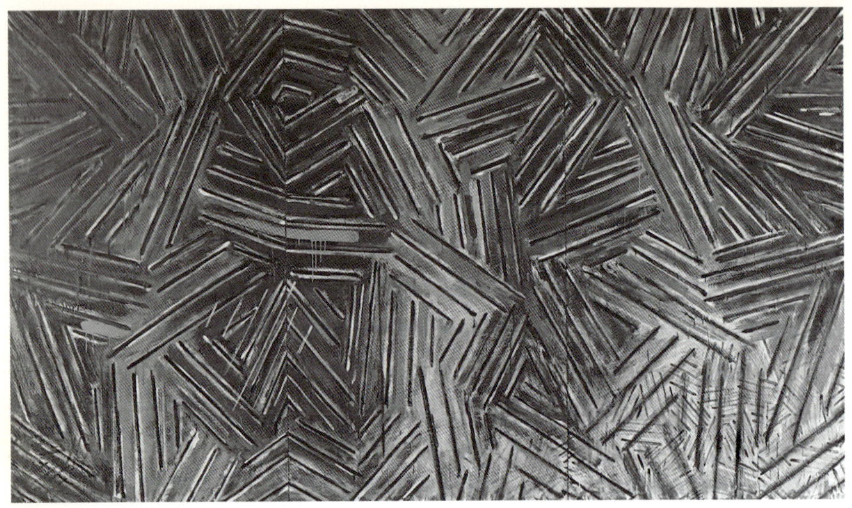

Between the Clock and the Bed, 1982–83, encaustic on canvas (three panels), 72 x 126 1/8 in.

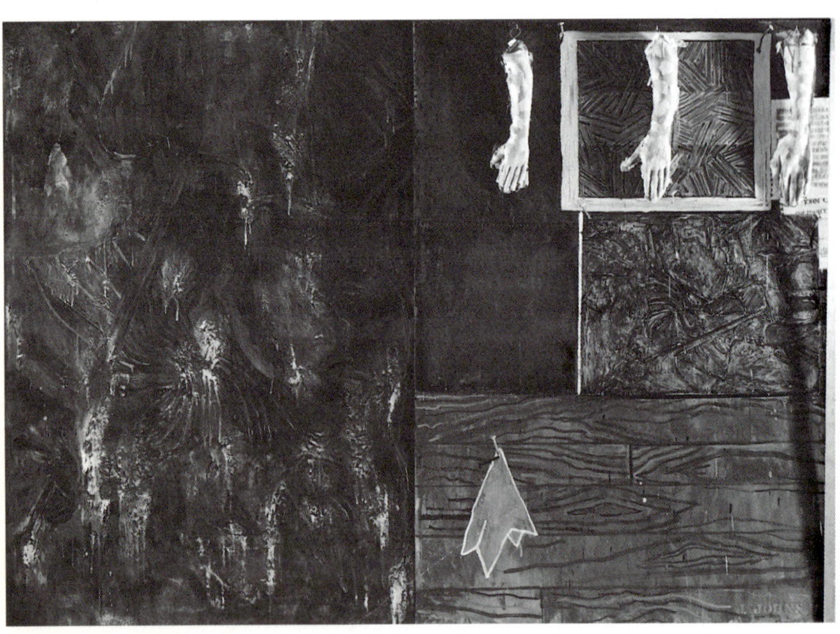

Perilous Night, 1982, encaustic on canvas with objects, 67 x 96 x 5 in.

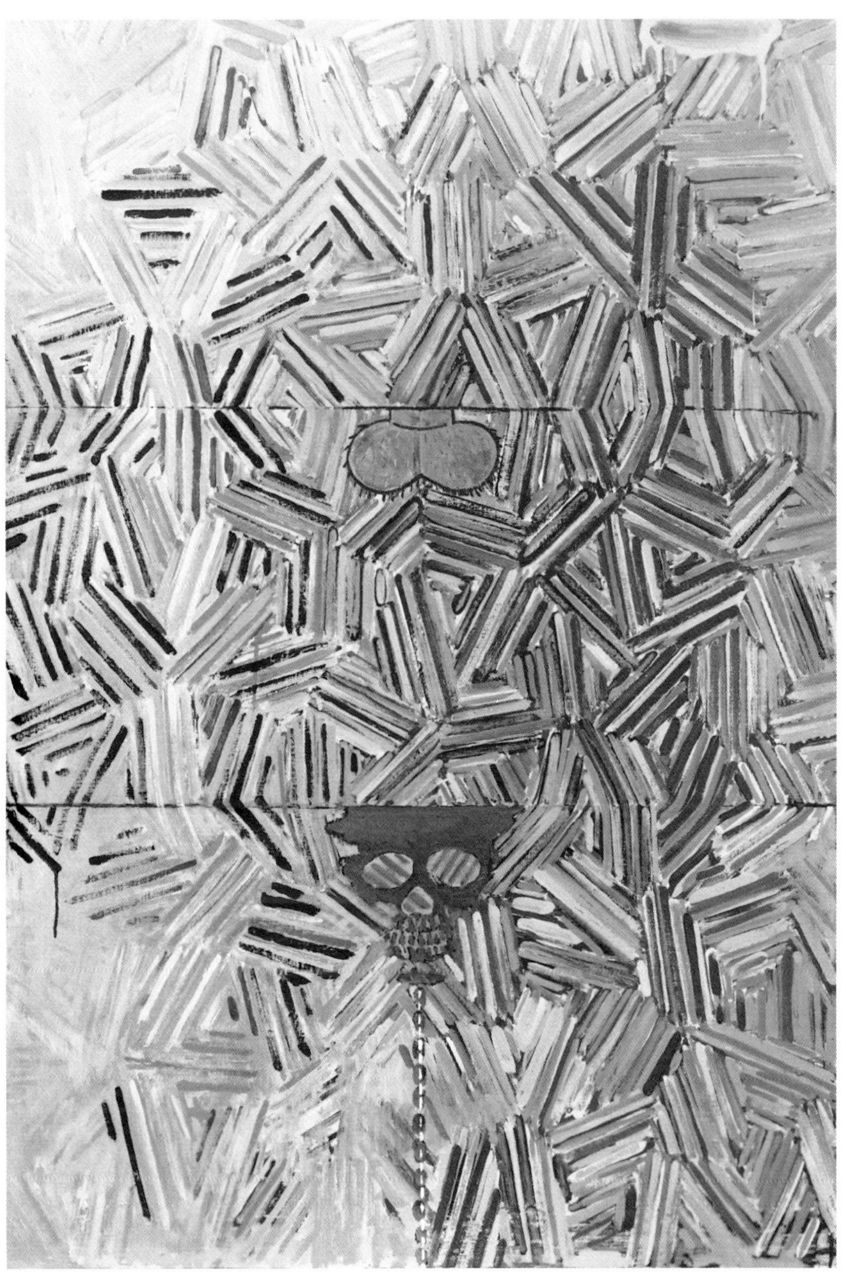

Tantric Detail I, 1980, oil on canvas, 50 1/8 x 34 1/8 in.

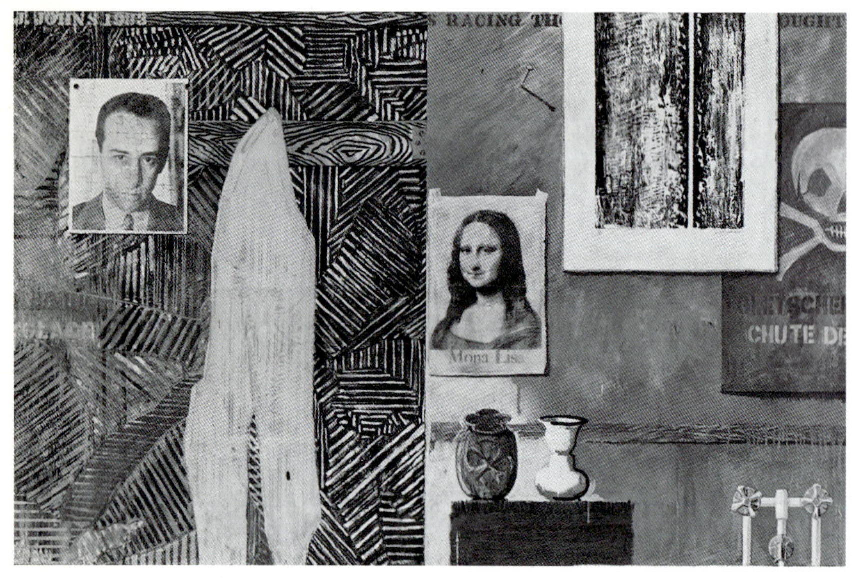

Racing Thoughts, 1983, encaustic and collage on canvas, 48 1/8 x 75 1/8 in.

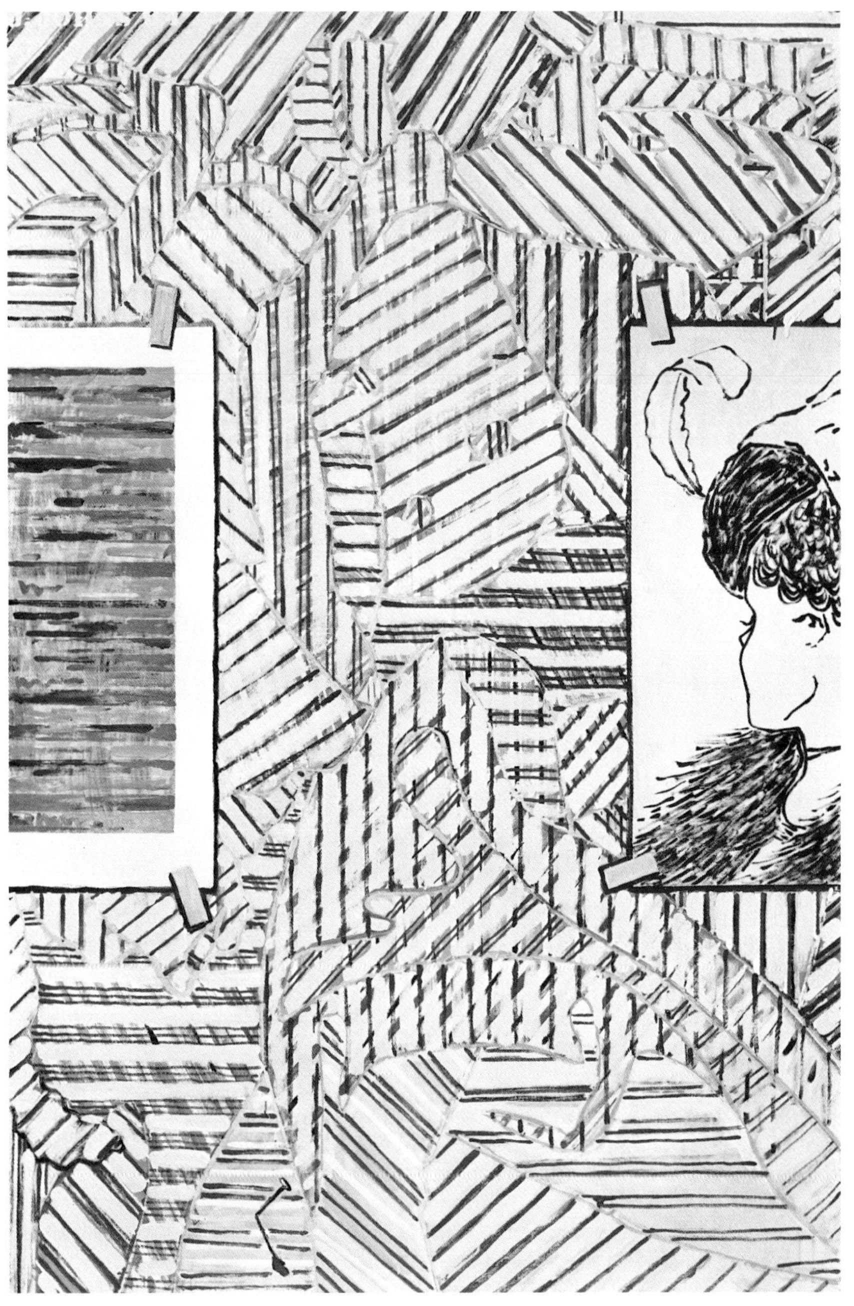

Untitled, 1984, oil on canvas, 75 x 50 in.

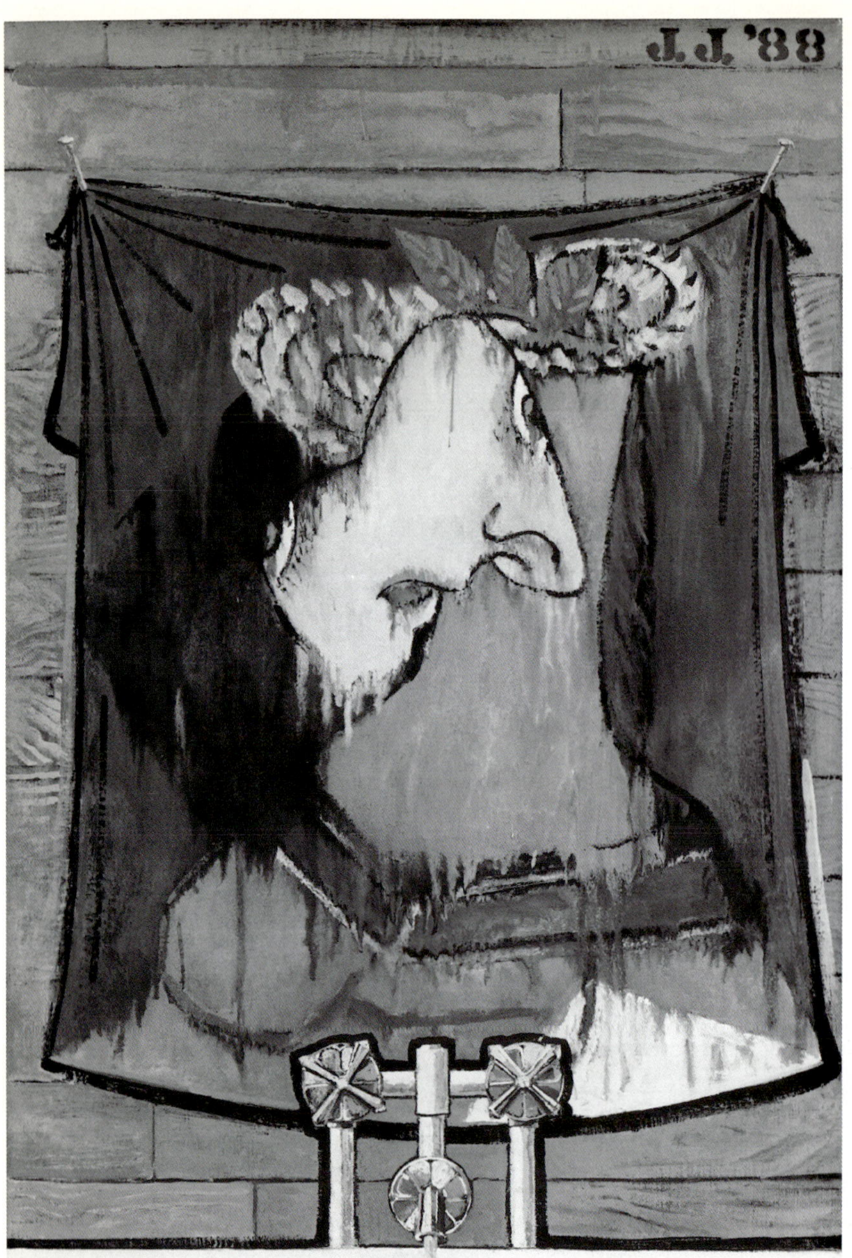

Untitled, 1988, encaustic on canvas, 38 x 26 in.

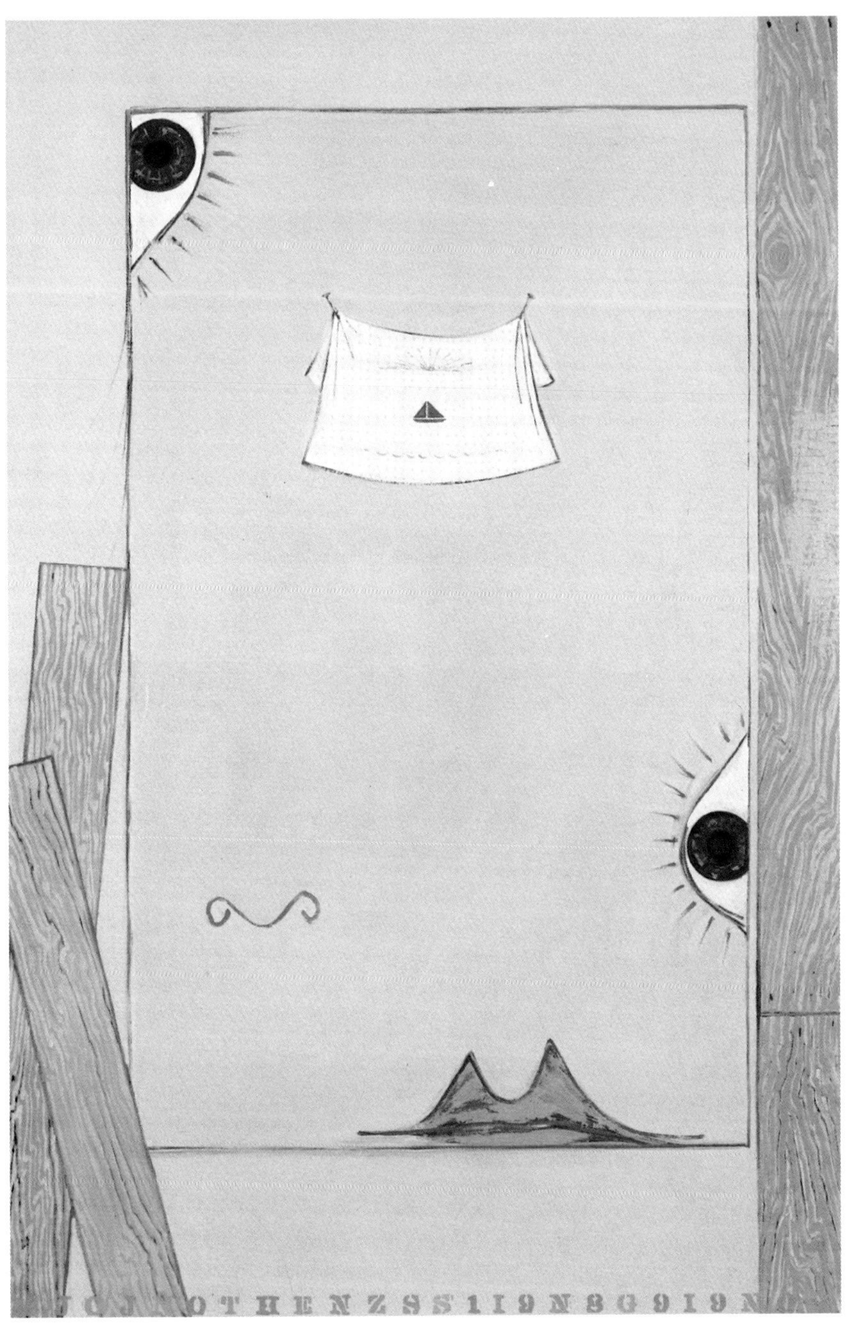

Montez Singing, 1989, oil on canvas, 76 x 50 in.

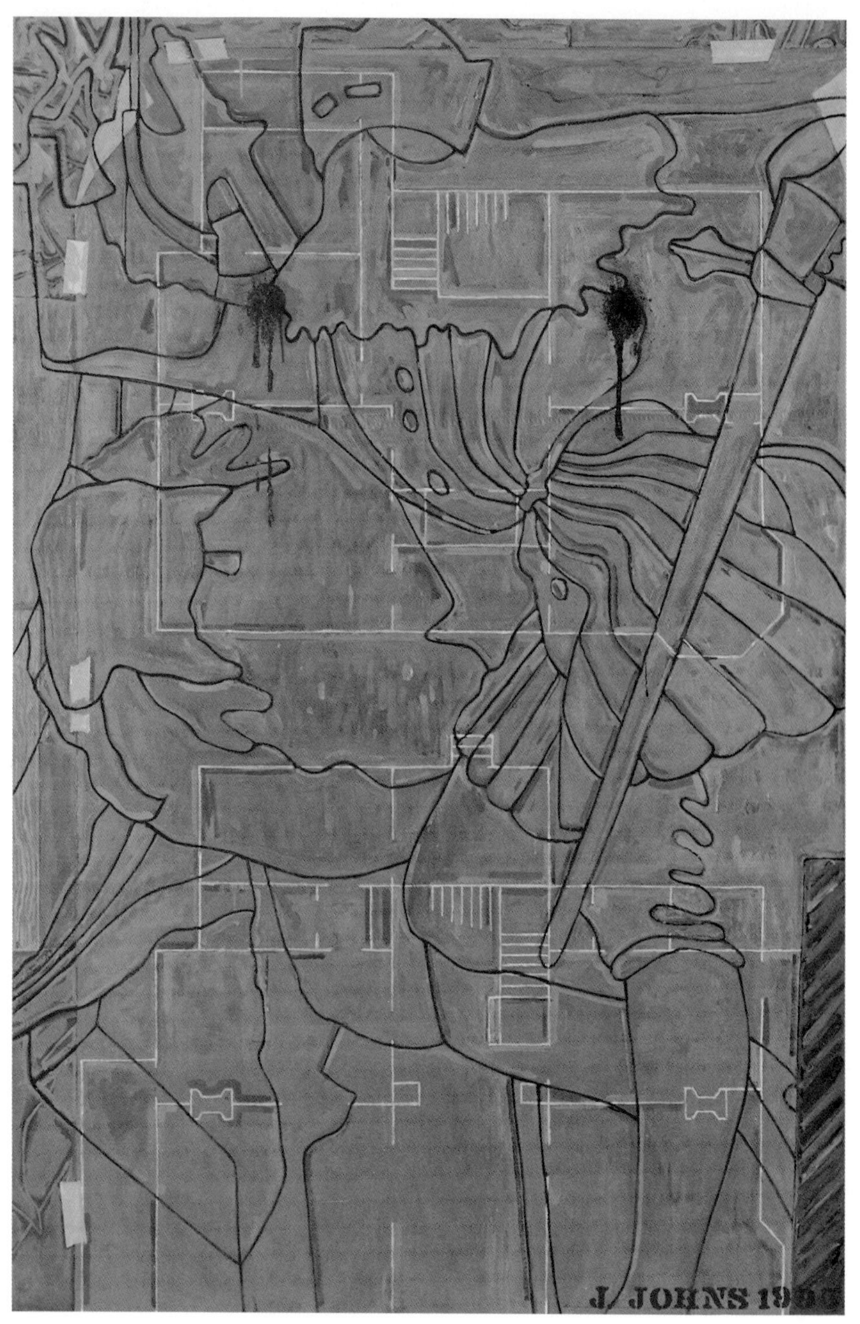

Untitled, 1995, oil on canvas, 66 x 44 in.

serving this tellingly ruthless gesture, the encaustic has eaten (taken into itself) and not eaten (not transformed it into waste) his bite. Johns has used encaustic to transform an action into an object. In the sculptural object, *The Critic Sees* (1961, sculptmetal on plastic on glass, 3 1/4 x 6 1/4 x 2 1/8 in., private collection, New York), Johns, in the Magritte tradition, placed an open mouth full of teeth behind each aperture of a pair of glasses. His antipathy toward critics, is clear; they eat art for their own needs and, in doing so, turn it into shit. For Johns seeing is not looking; it is blind consumption.

Why is looking a "trap"? Probably because it is the body (or one's eyes) which connects the individual to reality but the mind which makes the realization. After all, it was not until Johns made *Flag* that he gained insight into an entity he had seen many times before. For while the "watchman falls 'into' the 'trap' of looking," the "'spy' must be ready to 'move,' must be aware of his entrances and exits." The body sees, but the mind conceives of how to reconstruct that act. The "watchman" (body) is the one who brings Johns in contact with reality, while the "spy" (the mind) discovers something about their relationship to each other and to the world. The "watchman falls 'into'

---

necessary to fold the painting before taking a bite so that only his teeth marks would be evident. He pointed out, "You sometimes have to cheat a little in order to make something work."

the 'trap' of looking" because the act of looking, a bodily function, is what must be preserved by art; it must be eaten and not eaten by Johns's materials. The task of the spy is to find a way to resurrect the trapped body, thus earning it another, albeit temporary, guise.

When Johns wrote, "The spy designs himself to be overlooked," he was letting us know that art is finally not measured by the artist's intelligence. Yet, while the mind's ability to be self-reflective, to "remember" and "remember himself and his remembering" is a constant, often threatening attribute which can cut one off from the world of sensations, the mind is invisible. "I think," Descartes observed, "therefore I am," failing to take the body into account. "Beware of the body and the mind," Johns warned himself. "Avoid a polar situation." By Johns's measure a work of art which doesn't take into account the body, its production of waste, claims to exist outside the realm of human affairs, as if such a thing were possible.

When Johns wrote, "The watchman 'serves' as a warning," he proposed that the body will make the mind aware of time passing because it most likely will register time's effects before the mind does. "The watchman leaves his job and takes away no information," that is to say, the mind rather than the body remembers. If the body did the remembering, then the memory of the various pains we all have endured would be unbearable. But because the mind remembers, it must acknowledge the body's transformations. However, Johns also knows that the mind's capacity to remember can interfere with the body's ability to experience, that this is the polar situation which must be avoided.

Johns's figures of the watchman and spy enabled him to begin examining both his previous work and the present from another perspective; they formed a framework through which he could examine experience. These figures were both personae and alter egos; they had lives of their own. Beyond Johns's wanting to come up with a language that would adequately describe his experience, his primary reason for constructing these figures stemmed from a threefold desire: He wanted to remove himself as much as possible from the sphere of aesthetic considerations; he felt he had to give himself further permission to be true to what was "helpless" in his behavior; and he wanted to contextualize the behavioral properties of encaustic and bronze, materials with which he felt a deep affinity. The two most obvious inspirations behind Johns's personae are the writings of Ludwig Wittgenstein and Marcel Duchamp, both of which he had read closely by the early 1960s.

In *Philosophical Investigations*, which was published posthumously in 1953, Wittgenstein examined, among a range of topics, the relationship between subjective and objective experience. He was concerned with discovering the basis of knowledge; how does one know what one knows? In one passage he proposed the example of a man trying to corroborate his memory of the time a train departs by calling to mind an image of the timetable. Wittgenstein used this example to point out the fallacies such solipsistic thinking might lead to. He then reinforced his point with a metaphor: "As if someone were to buy several copies of the morning paper to assure himself what it said was true." Through these examples Wittgenstein was able to demonstrate that neither subjective nor objective truths are adequate measures of experience, and that one cannot rely on such measures to determine what one knows.

In his four-panel painting, *4 the News* (1962, encaustic and collage on canvas with objects, 65 x 50 1/4 in., private collection), which alludes to Wittgenstein's metaphor of the newspaper, Johns wedged a rolled-up newspaper between two panels and stenciled the painting's title and "Peto Johns" along the bottom. Paired with the so-called objective experience of the newspaper, Johns has registered one measure of subjective experience, a left handprint (he is right-handed). To left of the handprint and above the title Johns has stenciled the word THE twice*,

---

* Johns embedded the word *The* once before, in *The* (1957, encaustic on canvas, 24 x 20 in., private collection).

superimposing the smaller version over the larger one.

The doubling of the word *the* may have been inspired by the last line of Wallace Stevens's poem "The Man on the Dump":

> Where was it one first heard of the truth. The the.

As in Stevens's poem Johns's doubling of *the* proposes that there is no such thing as the truth, just "the the." Johns first read Stevens's poems when he was a teenager and made an etching more than three decades later in response to them.* The handprint embodies the limits of direct human experience, as opposed to the domain of consensus and ideals, which to some extent is embodied by the newspaper. By separating handprint and newspaper, Johns underscored his observation that

---

* In a conversation with the author, Johns said that he was given a book of Stevens's poetry in 1947 or '48. This suggests that the book was *Transport to Summer*, which was published in 1947. A third edition of *Harmonium*, Stevens's first book, which included "The Man on the Dump," was published in 1937. In 1985 the Arion Press published a limited edition of Stevens's poems on the thirtieth anniversary of his death. The poems were selected by Helen Vendler, who also wrote the introduction. Johns provided an etching for the frontispiece. Beginning early in his career with a drawing, *Tennyson* (1958, ink on paper, 11 5/8 x 8 3/4 in., collection the artist), Johns has alluded in his work to a number of poets and their work, among them Ted Berrigan, Hart Crane, and Frank O'Hara.

neither the body nor the mind alone can arrive at the truth; they must be made to work in tandem.

"Peto" alludes to the American trompe l'oeil artist John F. Peto (1854–1907), while *4 the News* is the first of a number of Johns's works to acknowledge Peto's painting *The Cup We All Race 4*, 1900.* Peto's painting depicts a trompe l'oeil dented tin cup hanging from a hook affixed to a "wooden panel." The title is painted as letters someone has gouged out of the "wooden frame" with a knife. Above the cup, and in the top section of the "wooden frame," Peto depicted a trompe l'oeil brass plate with his name stamped on it. The tin cup, wooden frame, brass nameplate, gouged letters—all the objects and surfaces in the composition—have been rendered into paint. For Johns, who had lavished equal care on his two sculptures titled *Painted Bronze* (both 1960), Peto's work must have come as a welcome revelation. By stenciling "Peto Johns" on the painting, Johns was defining the creator of the work as a synthesis of two different people. He and Peto are alter egos who made *4 the News*. In the guise of Peto, Johns,

---

* Johns learned of Peto's work from a reproduction that Ileana Sonnabend sent to him in the early 1960s. Among other things he would have noticed a number of affinities between paintings by Peto and Magritte; both men worked in a relatively straightforward, somewhat homely style, preferred a muted palette, and used trompe l'oeil devices to call reality into question.

who had not yet written “Sketchbook Notes,” found another way to contextualize a newspaper.

Although Duchamp’s name comes at the end of a list in “Sketchbook Notes,” his importance to Johns in both his art and his writing cannot be underestimated. In “The Creative Act,” a talk given in 1957, Duchamp proposed:

> Let us consider two important factors, the two poles of the creation of art: the artist on the one hand, and on the other the spectator who becomes posterity.
>
> To all appearances, the artist acts like a mediumistic being who, from the labyrinth beyond time and space, seeks his way to a clearing.
>
> If we give the attributes of a medium to the artist, we must deny him the state of consciousness on the aesthetic plane about what he is doing or why he is doing. All his decisions in the artistic execution of the work rest with pure intuition and cannot be translated into a self-analysis, spoken or written, or even thought out.
>
> T. S. Eliot, in his essay “Tradition and Individual Talent” writes: “The more perfect the artist, the more completely separate in him will be the man who suffers and the mind which creates; the more perfectly will the mind digest and transmute the passions which are its materials.”[8]

Certainly there is an affinity between Johns's "watchman" and Eliot's "man who suffers," and between the "spy" and the "mind which creates." Also, Johns's pairing of "eating" and not "eating" echoes Eliot's "digest" and "transmute." Johns's figures are a way of rejecting the unified "I" as the origin of his art; they exist in the third person and make art which comes from that place. Consequently, they are neither subjective nor objective in their intention but an unfixed, unpredictable combination of the two. At the same time Johns's figures can be seen as the counterparts of Duchamp's "artist" and "spectator," not the one who becomes "posterity" but the one who lives in time, amid change, the one who eats and is eaten.

The questions Johns tried to resolve in "Sketchbook Notes" are these: How do you define your existence in the world when your experience of it isolates you from others? How do you remain true to that fact of your existence, particularly when your work is placed before the public and is discussed by critics? How do you continue to focus on the actual when others claim you are not doing so? How do you remove yourself from the realm of aesthetic ideals, social pressures, and the audience's expectations, and go your own way? It is not Johns but the "watchman" who "falls 'into' the 'trap' of looking." And it is not Johns but the "spy" who "must remember and must remember himself and his remembering."*

By locating the origins of his art in the reciprocal relationship that arises in certain moments of looking, Johns was able to define himself as both spectator (watchman) and creator/destroyer (spy). In doing so he completed a circle between himself as maker and himself as viewer, which enabled him to jettison any residual dependency he might have on external standards of aesthetics and accomplishment.** Moreover, by connecting looking to eating and the cycle of consumption and waste, Johns not only further de-aestheticized looking and art making but also underscored art's connection to the body's passage toward dissolution.

The questions Johns resolved in "Sketchbook Notes" lead to others, one of them being: Where do the spy and

---

* In a conversation with Johns I once mentioned that when people came up to me after a poetry reading and commented on poems I had read, I felt as if they were talking about someone else and someone else's work. He responded, "They are."

** Although Johns was influenced by Duchamp's writings and art, in "Sketchbook Notes" he directly challenged Duchamp's belief that an individual's "decisions in the artistic execution of his work rest with pure intuition and cannot be translated into a self-analysis, spoken or written, or even thought out." Thus, rather than aligning himself with the avant-garde tradition which mystifies the artist's thinking, as Duchamp did, Johns attempts to demystify it without becoming reactionary, Newtonian, didactic, or simplistic.

watchman exist? Until the early 1980s the "continuity" underlying the "watchman," "the space," and "the objects" was more literal than pictorial, the connections existing within a narrower domain of experience. In *Map,* for example, Johns achieved a continuity among the collage fragments, the rectangles of primary color, the stenciled words, and the states' irregularly shaped rectangles, but all of them are derived from more closely related categories of existence. It was not until paintings such as *Racing Thoughts* (1983) that Johns achieved the desired "continuity" in a layered pictorial space occupied by items as diverse as a bathtub faucet, a jigsaw puzzle of his dealer, Leo Castelli, a reproduction of the *Mona Lisa,* a pair of corduroy pants, a highway warning in German and French, various pots, a laundry hamper, and a lithograph by Barnett Newman. In making images Johns switched from his unconventional method of applying encaustic to a more conventional one, a move he had been determined to complete since the beginning of his career.

For while it is clear that Johns achieved a continuity in early paintings such as *Flag,* where he collapsed a "flag" and collage fragments together, it was only after 1983 that he was able to bring a more unlikely and wider array of items together within the same layered pictorial space. The continuity he began achieving in *Racing Thoughts,* across the entire surface as well as from the front layers to the back, is more extensive and adept than at any previous point in his career.

If Johns was concerned with received knowledge, he would not have started working in a mode considered anti-modernist and thus obsolete: the depiction of space. After all, Johns is the artist who single-handedly introduced representation back into painting while completely emptying out the pictorial space. A flag, a surface, and an object became one. Now, instead of making airless, self-contained, autonomous paintings and objects, he works in a mode that is considered old-fashioned, if not outré. In doing so Johns challenges us to dispense with our aesthetic standards. At the same time he doesn't try to shock or titillate the viewers so much as to engage them, to compel them to look and examine. Reality rather than social or aesthetic codes is what he wants to touch; the rest is appearances. Reality will forever elude the individual who is satisfied with achieving fame in the social or aesthetic realm.

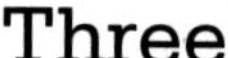

Three

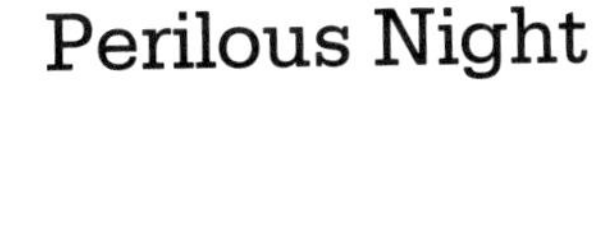

Perilous Night

"The spy," Johns wrote in the mid-1960s, "must be ready to 'move,' must be aware of his entrances and exits." This is the remark of someone reminding himself to be attentive to any possibility, yet also to be aware of how to seize the particular opportunity being afforded him. In the early 1980s Johns not only began jettisoning the crosshatch motif he had incorporated into his lexicon in the early '70s but also began embracing a more extensive vocabulary of objects. Johns's transition was not a sudden switch from one style, material, or subject to another but a carefully considered process in which entrances and exits (that is to say, passages from one realm to another) were carefully and publicly examined.

By 1983, when he finished the first *Racing Thoughts*, he had fully initiated a radically different phase in his work. Instead of re-membering (reconstructing) his perception of something, he began re-envisioning a wide array of articles taken directly from his life. Consequently, his recent paintings are based on a vision of reality that he can only make evident by locating and depicting disparate items within a complex pictorial structure which owes something to his reading of Cézanne: "each object reflecting the other." How, we must ask ourselves, did he move from one way of painting to another, from the transformation of a single object to the depiction of numerous items? And why?

An artist who became known in the late 1950s for his confounding transformations of objects associated with the beginning of socialization in childhood, who in the 1960s attached used objects, both domestic and from his studio, to painted surfaces, and who in the 1970s developed complex visual systems based on repeating and differentiating a crosshatch pattern within an all-over composition, Johns has entered a territory of painting few if any observers would have expected. At the very least, the differentiation of space within a pictorial structure has been considered outmoded since the late 1940s, when both Willem de Kooning and Jackson Pollock did their first breakthrough abstract paintings. Their all-over compositions (no beginning, no middle, and no end) and their emptying out of pictorial space seemingly rendered any use of the figure in a non-abstract space irrelevant because such painting would require that the artist develop a hierarchical composition. This is an assumption that Johns began overturning in *Racing Thoughts* (1983).

In his *Between the Clock and the Bed* paintings (1981–83), which allude to a late painting by Edvard Munch, Johns began underscoring his desire to "exit" from the crosshatch motif that had preoccupied him for nearly a decade. Done shortly before his death, Munch's *Between the Clock and the Bed* (1940–1942, oil on canvas, 59 x

47 ¼ in., Munchmuseet, Oslo) depicts the aged artist standing between a grandfather clock and a small single bed. Behind him on the wall are a number of "paintings," presumably his, and a doorway opening onto a sunlit room, probably the artist's studio. Munch has stepped out of his bright studio into a darkened room. His paintings are behind him, both compositionally and literally. Art, Munch's painting makes clear, becomes part of its time, as well as part of one's past, but time is always present and continuous. Caught in time, one lives between the past and the future, between the after (time started) and the before (time stopped).

Johns began his *Between the Clock and the Bed* paintings shortly after seeing Munch's painting and recognizing that his own crosshatch pattern very closely resembled the red, yellow, and blue cross-hatching of the Lapland coverlet Munch depicted on his bed. For although Munch used the crosshatch some three decades before Johns introduced it into his vocabulary in the left panel of a four-panel painting, *Untitled* (1972, oil, encaustic, and collage on canvas with objects, 72 x 192 in., Museum Ludwig, Cologne), Johns had been using it for nearly a decade before he saw Munch's self-portrait.

In all three of his three-panel paintings, Johns juxtaposed at least two different-size crosshatch patterns, one extending across the entire composition and the other confined to a smaller area, usually the lower right-hand corner. Thus in all three of his paintings, Johns has placed a smaller-scale pattern in the same area where Munch depicted his bed; and in the first two of his paintings Johns painted the smaller pattern in primary colors, deliberately echoing Munch's palette. Each panel echoes one of three elements in Munch's painting.

Alluding to the source within the crosshatch is something Johns did before, in his three-panel painting *Weeping Women* (1975, encaustic and collage on canvas, 50 x 102 1/4 in., Mr. and Mrs. S. I. Newhouse Collection, New York), in which he combined crosshatching, impressions made from an iron and circles from a tin can, melted encaustic, and white lines to convey an abstracted figure.* Having made an equation between "encaustic" and "flesh," Johns uses his vocabulary to make a painting that is both a surface and layered composition (something he started with *Flag*). One has the feeling that a figure is entangled in the web of crosshatching, and neither figure nor surface finally subsumes the other.

---

* In a conversation with the author, Johns mentioned a story he had heard about Picasso. Evidently, when Picasso saw de Kooning's "Woman" paintings for the first time, he said, "Melted Picasso." In the middle (ocher) panel of *Weeping Women*, Johns pressed a hot iron into the encaustic surface, both leaving an impression and causing the wax to run.

In 1937 Picasso did three versions of *Weeping Women*, one primarily in red, another in ocher, and a third in blue. The predominant color in each of the three panels in Johns's painting echoes one of Picasso's versions. While many observers feel that Johns's allusions are part of an elusive, overly intellectual game he plays with the viewer, his real reason, again, is to define a visual duality in which the viewer is compelled to shift between looking at the entire painting while missing what is embedded within it. For Johns no view of reality is comprehensive, thus he allows the viewer no fixed place from which to come in complete visual contact with the entire painting.

At the same time, Johns wondered if there was a way he could make the image (figure) and the pattern (ground) simultaneously visible. Between *Weeping Women* (1975) and the first *Between the Bed and the Clock*, Johns did a drawing, *Untitled* (1978, watercolor, graphite pencil, and ink on paper, 17 15/16 x 17 1/4 in., collection of Mr. and Mrs. Larry Wolf), in which he wrote and underlined "Husk," "Locust," and "Cicada" on the side margin. This was followed by a drawing and a number of paintings titled *Cicada*, an insect that periodically and only briefly emerges from a long dormancy. For Johns, who had used encaustic to preserve pieces of newspaper, making the paint a kind of husk, the issue was clear: Is it possible to make what is buried inside the beeswax break out of its shell? Can what the encaustic has eaten and not eaten be made more visible? How much can be located on the surface when reality itself is shifting and layered?

Underlying these questions is Johns's desire to shift from the unconventional manner of his early work to a more conventional, though no less radical manner. Whereas Duchamp turned his back on painting, Johns has deepened his investigations of its capacity to embody and convey meaning. In choosing "Cicada" as a title, Johns underscored a link between the beeswax and the insect. Both bees and cicadas secrete a material which they use to build a hive or husk. Clearly Johns wanted to expose some aspect of himself, and his distinct though connected states, to the viewer. But in order to take that risk, he had to find both an "exit" and an "entrance."

Tantric Detail I (1980, oil on canvas, 50 1/8 x 34 1/8 in., collection the artist) is Johns's attempt to develop pictorial images that correspond to his separate states. Two other *Tantric Detail* paintings (both 1981) would follow. All of them are divided into three equal-size horizontal sections, each of which has been delineated by a crosshatch pattern. At the juncture between one section and another, Johns changed the direction of the crosshatching but not necessarily the color. At the same time, at the juncture between the top and middle sections, Johns depicted a hairy scrotum topped by a rounded penile shaft, which has been cut off by the border and which seems to be slipping beneath the adjacent plane just above it. In the bottom panel Johns depicted the flattened image of a skull, its top devoured by the delineated area above it. The placement of the penile shaft and the skull implies three movements: up, down, and into.

The penile shaft and skull evoke a bodiless figure. Because the skull has been placed beneath the testicles, and because of the stylistic differences in their depiction, the viewer should not assume that these elements are aspects of a single figure. While the skull and testicles are familiar signs for death and creation, by now we have learned that the simplest or quickest reading of Johns's art is likely to be the least rewarding.

In all the *Tantric Detail* paintings, Johns combined figural elements and patterning to investigate, as well as to contextualize, the relationship between figure and ground. His interest here in a figure/ground relationship runs counter to much of his earlier work. However, instead of juxtaposing a fixed figure against a stable ground, as is done in traditional paintings, Johns took two extreme images and not only placed them both within and against a shifting pattern of crosshatches but differentiated between them stylistically.

In *Flag*, Johns stripped away the historical and social meanings surrounding "United States," bringing the phrase closer to its essential meaning. In calling attention to the separate existence of the letters, he directed our attention toward the way a word as individual letters mirrors the union of separate states that constitute one's isolated existence. In the three *Tantric Detail* paintings, he extricated the figure/ground relationship from its art historical meanings and nudged it closer to its essential meaning. Each of us is a figure whose fate is inextricably bound up with the ground (earth).*

Throughout his career Johns has used various materials to both eat and not eat an object's essential features. Although he may have derived the cartoony image of the penile shaft and hairy balls from a specific source, that source is not apparent. This marks a significant shift in Johns's career, since he is not an inventive artist but a transformative one; he recontextualizes pre-existing images and articles. At the same time Johns has repeatedly used his materials to eat (destroy) and not eat (preserve and transform) aspects of the world he inhabits. The positioning of the testicles and skull evokes Johns's asso-

---

* Johns further underscored this reading of the figure/ground relationship in his paintings of the "Seasons," where he depicted his shadow contiguous with the paintings' ground and included a number of optical images that shift between figure and ground. Johns derived the image of his shadow by having a friend draw the outline of his actual shadow on a large sheet of paper placed on the ground.

ciations of destroying and preserving with eating and not eating. We read the skull as being "devoured" and the penile shaft as "penetrating" the area above it. Finally, just as cicadas and bees create but cannot preserve themselves, encaustic (or "flesh") cannot create and preserve itself. The "watchman's" residency in encaustic is temporary. Once a work of art is made, the artist faces the same dilemma: What do I do now?

The flat image of the skull and the rounded image of the testicles literally exist in separate states and in this regard evoke *Target with Plaster Casts* (1955, encaustic and collage on canvas with objects, 51 x 44 in., private collection). Working right after he finished *Flag*, Johns constructed a row of nine compartments, which he attached to an encaustic painting of a bull's-eye in primary colors. In each compartment he placed a different-colored plaster cast of a body part, including a penis, an ear, a hand, a foot, a nipple, and the mouth and nose of a face. One compartment he left empty, and in the remaining two he placed unidentifiable parts.

Whereas the "united states" of the individual were the central focus of *Flag*, the disunity of these states was foremost in Johns's mind both when he constructed *Target with Plaster Casts* and when he painted the *Tantric Detail* paintings. "Will the spy and watchman ever meet?" he asked. From works done nearly three decades apart, one concludes that Johns believes such a meeting is unlikely. The mind and body seldom if ever function in harmony.

Johns divided *Perilous Night* (1982, encaustic on canvas with objects, 67 x 96 x 5 in., private collection) into two equal-size sections, both vertical. The title comes from a 1943 composition by John Cage, whose cover sheet and first page Johns silkscreened along the right edge of his painting, near the top. *Perilous Night*—or perilous knight—the pun within the title alerts the viewer to the painting's subject, the inextricable link between one's body and one's passage in time. At the same time, the title alludes to the night Johns dreamed he was painting an American flag. Also, while the knight or the "watchman falls 'into' the trap of 'looking,'" "the spy must be ready to 'move,' must be aware of his entrances and exits." One cannot make the same work again, one must move on, and acknowledge time's passing.

On the left side Johns both isolated and transformed a detail from the right panel of Matthias Grünewald's *Isenheim Altarpiece* (1512–1515). The detail is of two knights who have fallen asleep in front of Jesus' sarcophagus. In the original there are three knights, but Johns's detail is of the two in the foreground. Jesus is rising from the grave, and the immense force of this miraculous event has knocked the soldiers down, causing their helmets to slip over their eyes. They are present at the Resurrection, but they do not witness it: “The watchman leaves his job & takes away no information.”

Johns’s outline of the knights physically and visually articulates the limitations of the body, which experiences reality but doesn’t necessarily comprehend or remember it. Memory and judgment, after all, are the mind’s functions, and recalling the source of *Flag,* it was the “spy” (mind) who remembered the dream, not the “watchman.” The detail is a magenta outline that is contiguous with, but separate from, the black background. Johns rotated the detail so that it appears as if the knights are falling both down and into the uneven encaustic surface. At the same time Johns in places reheated the encaustic to such an extent that the black wax has started to drip. Thus, the dripping wax and the falling figures echo not only each other but a state of helplessness.

The right side is where the “spy” is considering the entrances and exits that can be taken. At the far right edge Johns attached a stick that extends into the viewer’s space as well as casts a shadow on the painting, indicating that the artist hasn’t completely jettisoned real space for illusionistic or pictorial space. Along the top of the painting, Johns attached three casts of blotched or “camouflaged” arms. The left one is topped with red, the middle one with yellow, and the right one with blue. Camouflage, the viewer recognizes, is one method of making a figure and the background blend together.

The red-topped (or leftmost) arm rests against the wall. Some spots of red are visible below it, both on the dark green wall and on the trompe l'oeil gray wood paneling directly beneath the wall. Beneath the blue-topped arm are the silk-screened "pages" of Cage's composition, while beneath the middle or yellow-topped arm Johns depicted a trompe l'oeil drawing "pinned" to the wall. The "shadows" cast by the nails are mirrored in the real shadow cast by the stick.

Both the crosshatch pattern and the colors of the trompe l'oeil drawing echo the first two *Between the Clock and the Bed* paintings, but there are also telltale differences. The arm both covers and forms a juncture between the drawing's left and right sides. Thus the left side is divided into three stacked rectangles which, in descending order, are green, orange, and violet; on the right side this order is reversed. In its combination of continuity and discontinuity, the drawing embodies an unanswerable question: Does change require rupture or is it that rupture necessitates change? This is one of the questions Johns must answer in *Perilous Night,* as he moves from one kind of painting to another.

Directly beneath the trompe l'oeil drawing and the collaged pages of Cage's composition, which it partly covers, is a trompe l'oeil drawing of the two knights done in grisaille. In this case Johns has correctly aligned the drawing, so that the knights' position conforms to the one they have in Grünewald's painting. Because their bodies are also the same color as the ground, they too have fallen into the paint. Below the grisaille drawing, and taking up the entire breadth of the right side, is a gray trompe l'oeil wood panel wall to which a grayish handkerchief outlined in white has been pinned.

Here Johns has transformed the flag, its "broad stripes and bright stars," into an illusionistic trompe l'oeil depiction of a wall made up of wide planks with rippling wood grain (stripes), to which a blank handkerchief (the flag's canton) has been pinned. The starless "handkerchief" is bidding adieu to itself; it is also an image of surrender and grief.* Near the handkerchief is a drip of red paint; elsewhere on the gray wall are drips of yellow and blue. Johns knew he had to say good-bye to the ways of painting that had preoccupied him for much of his career if he was going to depict objects within a pictorial space. The difference between the right and left sides of *Perilous Night* is that the former is layered illusionistically (the handkerchief pinned to the wall) and literally (the arm attached to the wall), while the figural outline depicted in

* In *Weeping Women* (1975), Johns included an outline of the woman crying into a handkerchief that Picasso depicted.

the latter is contiguous with the painting's ground.

The watchman (or body) may have fallen into the paint, but the spy has seen a way to release (or resurrect) him from the trap of looking. Through his recontextualization of various flat articles, such as drawings and a handkerchief, which, like a flag, is a piece of cloth, the spy has found both an entrance and an exit. He knows that making these transitions is filled with perils, one of which is that he (the mind) cannot become too isolated from the watchman (the body). "Avoid a polar situation," Johns wrote nearly two decades earlier.

Four

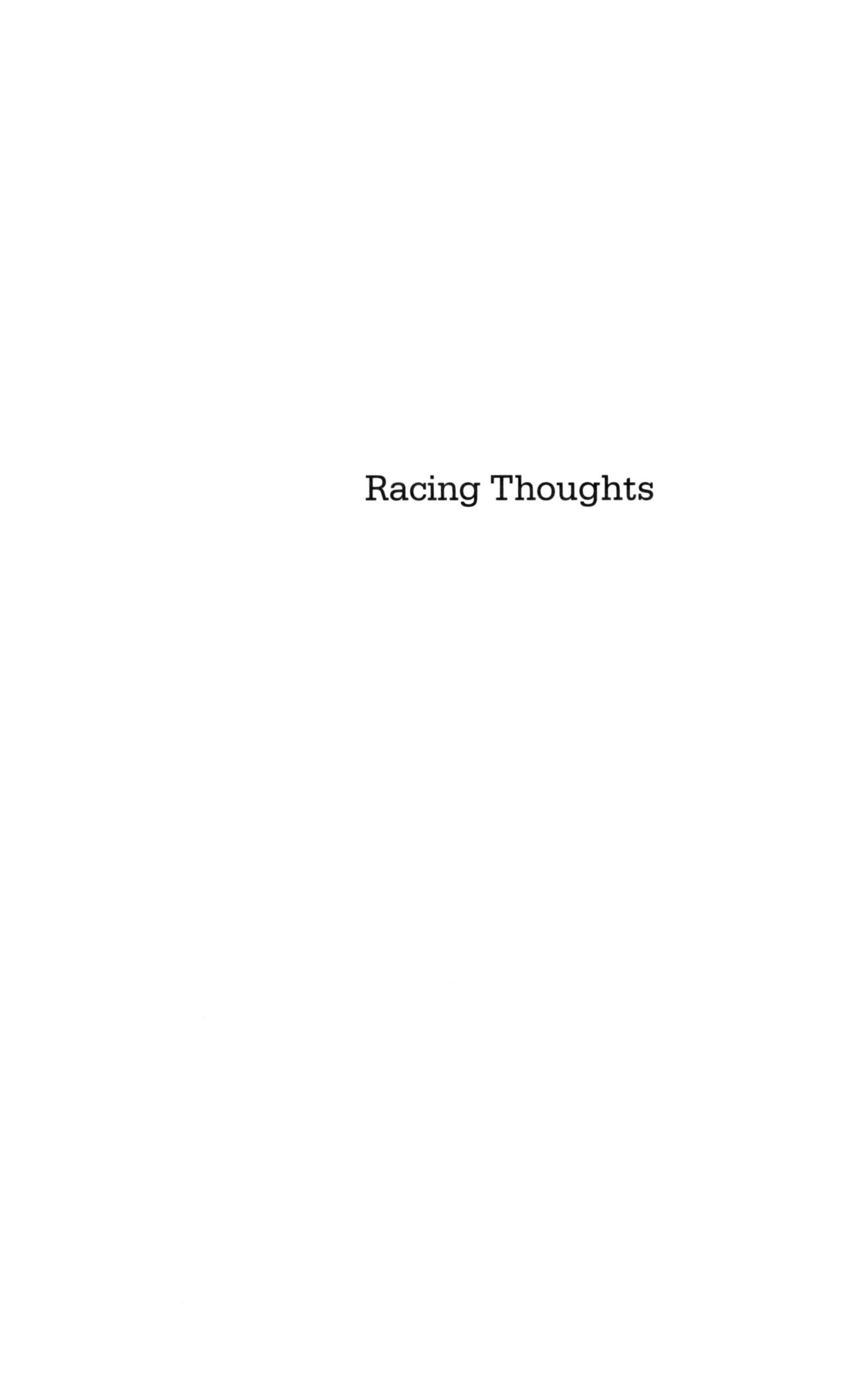

Racing Thoughts

Racing Thoughts (1983) is based on the split perception that occurs when one is taking a bath, with the head above the body, immersed in water. It marks not only Johns's exit from the all-over paintings that preoccupied him through much of the 1970s but also his complete entrance into a new phase of painting, which is the depiction of different, carefully arranged articles within a relatively straightforward, layered pictorial space. Instead of preserving a "flag," his paintings would now consist of trompe l'oeil images of actual things. For despite their variousness all the items in the paintings have their counterparts in reality. In order to bring these different objects together, Johns had to structure a perceptual continuum of distinct phases which would flow together. In this regard his recent paintings extend out of the layered compressions he achieved in *Flag* and *Map*.

As in *Flag*, where the newspaper collage and the flag's design compel the viewer to shift between looking and reading, the continuum Johns desired had to be open-ended. At the same time, in contrast to his earlier work, Johns wanted this perceptual experience to occur entirely on the surface. Formally, this is what separates *Racing Thoughts* from his earlier work. He has accumulated a vocabulary in which each object embodies a distinct visual experience, which he uses to structure a multi-layered, open-ended narrative.

Racing Thoughts synthesizes all of Johns's thinking about the body-mind relationship, and the relationships of body and mind to reality that he so carefully described in the middle paragraph of "Sketchbook Notes." The painting embodies Johns's vision of the body and mind in legible objects that have come into his possession; it acknowledges time's passing as well as the consequences of that passing; it pays homage to various individuals who have influenced his public and private or artistic life; it examines a moment of crisis, when one's racing thoughts (the mind) are on the brink of both separating the mind from the body and propelling the individual toward solipsism.

The composition of *Racing Thoughts* is invented rather than given. The painting is divided into two equal-size sections, which roughly correspond to the rustic bathroom of a house in upstate New York that Johns owned at the time. The left side is a trompe l'oeil depiction of a door with two horizontal wooden boards, while the right side is of a wall with the rim of a bathtub visible along the right side of the bottom edge. Extending from behind the tub's front edge is a wicker laundry hamper on which Johns has depicted two pots, one commemorating the Silver Jubilee of Queen Elizabeth II and the other made by the eccentric American ceramicist George Ohr. By dividing the composition into two equal, adjacent areas, one a "door" and the other the "room" with a bathtub, Johns alerts us that the painting focuses on the shifting bonds between the artist's public and private lives.

The site of the painting is a room with a bath, where one immerses the body in water, naked and alone. The inspiration for the bath came from Frida Kahlo's painting *What the Water Showed Me* (1938), which depicts scenes from the artist's life reflected on the bathwater's surface. Looking down at the water and her body, of which the viewer sees only her toes, Kahlo reflects upon her life. Johns saw Kahlo's painting shortly before he began *Racing Thoughts*.[9] In addition, there is an anecdote about Picasso that Johns knows well and that has, by his own admission, amused and haunted him for years. Evidently, Picasso was surprised that when people take baths, they don't melt, like sugar cubes.[10]

Alluding once again to Peto's *The Cup We All Race 4*, Johns has stenciled RACING THOUGHTS in capital letters along the top of the right panel. THOUGHTS is divided into TH and OUGHT by Johns's trompe l'oeil image of *Untitled*, a 1961 lithograph by Barnett Newman, which Johns depicted with its top margin cut off by the painting's edge. The S has been placed on the right side's far left edge, in front of "RACING." Thus, the viewer reads: S RACING TH OUGHT. At the same time, punning on his earlier admonition to "avoid a polar situation," along the painting's right edge Johns depicted a Swiss highway warning sign, whose German and French phrases can be translated "beware of falling ice." Having entered a new phase in his career, Johns's mind is racing with excitement and nervousness.

The issue he faces is not to let his excitement interfere with his thinking; he must be vigilant in making sure that "the spy stations himself to observe the watchman." Aligned along the right edge, the Swiss sign, with its skull and crossbones, is directly above the faucet and rim of the tub. Cropped by the painting's right edge, the French and German phrases, but not the skull and crossbones, extend in from the left side of the painting. If we connect both the title and the warnings, the painting becomes two cylinders, with the right (or private) side curled inside the left (or public) side.

Having once embedded pieces of printed matter within encaustic, Johns has now exposed fragments of printed matter (among them, the Newman lithograph and the highway sign) to the public, made them more visible. Thus, on the right side, in addition to the bathtub with faucet and handles, laundry hamper, two pots, highway warning and Newman lithograph, Johns depicted two other images. One is a trompe l'oeil nail (and its shadow) below RACING and between the edge of the patterned left side and the Newman lithograph. The other is a poster of the *Mona Lisa* "taped" to the wall below the nail and directly above the Ohr pot.

On the left side of the painting, Johns used a contour line to depict a surface made up of irregularly shaped, interlocking pieces, each of which has been delineated by crosshatching. Where the contoured pieces meet, the crosshatching may change direction or be disrupted, with the strokes in one demarcated area having no connection with those adjacent to it. Johns's combination of striations and contours evokes a collision between two-dimensionality and three-dimensionality, between surface and form. Though the relationship is not immediately obvious, the composition of the door is based on the boil-covered demon in the *Temptation of Saint Anthony* panel of Grünewald's Isenheim Altarpiece. The "watchman" has fallen further into the paint, and the feverish demon becomes linked with both the heated encaustic and the hot bath. Johns's reluctance to make the body visible is based not on his shyness but on his recognition that a fixed image of one's body betrays the flux of reality. Thus, only the "spy" (or mind) can make its "remembering" visible.

On top of this pattern of interlocking pieces Johns depicted two different-size horizontal boards complete with wood grain. On the lower board, and at the far right edge, where the left and right sides meet, he depicted a trompe l'oeil hinge which in terms of the composition serves two functions: it underscores the folding and unfolding that occurs in the mind's eye when the viewer correctly aligns the title and the highway warning, and it conveys that the patterned left side of the painting can be read as a "door" on which two items have been suspended: a jigsaw puzzle portrait of Leo Castelli, Johns's dealer, and a pair of tan corduroy pants. At the same time, Johns has undermined this reading by extending the demarcating lines of the interlocking pieces over the "wood grain," which causes the viewer to shift attention from all-over patterning to layered space and back again, a shift that recalls the compacted, unsystematic construction of *Flag* and *Map*.

Along the top of the left side, near the right edge, in the area defined by the "wooden" board, Johns stenciled in capital letters "J. JOHNS" and "1983," the year he completed the painting. Below his signature, the Castelli jigsaw puzzle and the tan pants hint at a body that is unseen. The jigsaw puzzle is a cracked surface, evoking rupture's inevitability; it is also an irregular grid, echoing both the door and the structured placement of articles on the right side or wall.

Whereas the knights on the left side of *Perilous Night* have fallen into the paint, in *Racing Thoughts* the falling is both completed and anticipated. The susceptibility of encaustic to extreme cold is evoked in the warning:

beware of falling ice. Thus, on the left side, where Castelli's fissured face has been placed, the warning is addressed to the painting's owner: please protect from extreme states. Within this context the fallen "watchman" or boil covered demon conveys the body's vulnerability to extremes of temperature and the passing of time.

On this and numerous other levels, *Racing Thoughts* speaks of its own vulnerability and impending loss. If the ice has started to fall, then the cracking of the encaustic (which the puzzle pieces evoke) would be a sign that it is too late. For Johns has also established a visual echo between the jigsaw portrait and the interlocking pieces constituting the door. Has the "watchman" fallen into the paint, leaving only his fissured face and pants? The combination of patterning (flatness) and rotation (dimensionality) that Johns used to delineate the door certainly suggests this possibility. Or is the portrait one of the spy's guises? Mustn't the spy (or the figural elements on the painting's right side) guard against becoming too separate from the watchman? Certainly, Johns's "spy" is evoked in the puzzle portrait; "the spy," Johns wrote, "stations himself to observe the watchman," anticipating as well as echoing both the perceptual split one has when taking a bath and the placement of the Leo Castelli portrait puzzle above the patterned door.

Within "beware of falling ice," one hears two other

possible warnings: beware of failing eyes, and beware of falling "I's." The "watchman" may have fallen into the paint, but the "spy" should be careful not to shed too many of his guises because there is no originating one. In moving from the impersonal realm of "maps" to a room in one's own house, Johns knew that he could not succumb to the power of memory and personal associations, that he had to be as rigorous in his examination of his thoughts as he was of the flag. Again the bodiless puzzle portrait of Castelli (one of the spy's guises) comes into play. However, lest we become too dependent on "Sketchbook Notes," I should point out that Johns's writings serve an auxiliary function, and that he established in the painting a dense, self-contained series of visual experiences. Once the viewer recognizes that *Racing Thoughts* mirrors the relationship of mind and body that occurs when taking a bath, the painting begins to reveal its meanings. Thus the jigsaw puzzle defines one understanding of that experience and the distribution of the painting's title another.

On the right side, the three items that have been "attached" to the wall are the *Mona Lisa* "poster," the Newman "lithograph," and the highway warning, in that order. The original Newman lithograph, *Untitled,* 1961, consists of two heavily scumbled fields divided into two-thirds and one-third areas by a sharp vertical "zip." Johns kept the compositional format of the "lithograph" but positioned it so that the top white border is cropped by the painting's top edge. In his lithographs Newman considered the white border an "intrusion" and thought that it should be dealt with as part of the composition. Johns's Newman "lithograph" clues us to the fact that the positive and negative spaces of the painting, which can be translated into the objects "affixed" to the wall and the closed and open rectangles formed by their placement, are of equal importance. Thus, the right side isn't made up of objects attached to a picture plane or wall. Rather, the wall or picture plane has been transformed into interlocking pieces, each of which embodies a distinct visual experience linked to those around it. Thus, there is an open square formed by extending the bottom edge of the Newman lithograph, the right edge of the *Mona Lisa* poster, and the left edge of the highway warning. The bottom of the square is delineated by the trompe l'oeil wood wainscotting extending across the wall. In this regard, the right side echoes the jigsaw portrait puzzle which, in turn, echoes the patterned wall on which it is mounted. At the same time, by making an empty square a central part of the right side's composition, Johns alludes to Cézanne, who in many of his late paintings defined an empty square rectangle near the center of his compositions.

The Newman "lithograph" is the only object that extends past the painting's top edge; the pants, laundry hamper, and tub extend below the bottom edge. All of them have to do with the body, either covering it or cleaning it. Despite the cropping, the image in Newman's "lithograph" remains in full view. Because Newman is noted for his non-objective, abstract paintings with religious themes, his "lithograph" conveys through its position a number of meanings, one of them that existence curtails transcendence. Johns's cropping underscores that transcendence can be depicted but that it exists outside the realm of direct experience. The vertical "zip" not only divides Newman's composition into proportionally related areas but, if extended, would divide the right side of Johns's painting into two unequal though related areas.

Of all the negative spaces defined by the poster, lithograph, and highway sign, only one is a completely closed rectangle. This rectangle is delineated by the right edge of the Newman "lithograph," the top edge of the highway warning, and the top and right edges of the painting; it is defined both illusionistically and literally. Along the top of the rectangle is stenciled the word OUGHT. Initially, OUGHT suggests that Johns felt he was under a moral obligation to make each part of the painting, its negative and positive spaces, of equal importance. He was trying to uphold his reading of Cézanne, "each object reflecting the other." This urgency is underscored by the rectangle itself and the way it fits into the composition. It is located in the upper right-hand corner; its height (8 in.) is one-sixth of the painting's while its width (6 1/4 in.) is one-twelfth of the painting's.

As part of the title, OUGHT or the figure 0 becomes one of the destinations toward which Johns's mind is racing. By placing the figure 0 in a rectangle, whose size is integral to the composition, Johns has reminded us that the nothing, infinity, and other abstract concepts began with the introduction of zero into the number system. By placing the figure 0 next to the Newman lithograph, which is adjacent to an open, rectangular section of wall in which someone has "hammered" a nail, Johns has aligned three ways of understanding time passing.

The trompe l'oeil nail evokes both absence and something about to happen. The asymmetrical composition of Newman's lithograph evokes movement rather than stasis. The proportional shift directs our attention toward the adjacent rectangle and the figure 0. Around the time Newman was working on *Untitled*, he was also working on a series of fourteen paintings which he would collectively title "The Stations of the Cross," whose composition was based on his knowledge of the Cabala.[11] Newman believed it is possible to hint at spiritual presence through the materiality of art, whereas Johns uses art to understand his relationship to materiality. Thus, Johns cojoined the Newman "lithograph" with the figure 0 in order to evoke their mutually exclusive beliefs. By using the Newman "lithograph" to split THOUGHT into TH and OUGHT Johns was suggesting that all thinking eventually leads to being conscious of one's mortality. At the same time, he stenciled "J. JOHNS" in a position which mirrors his positioning of OUGHT. It is his own absence that he was making visible, for Johns knows that in time, he will become the figure 0, will become his art (Johns first incorporated numerals into his art in 1955). Finally, OUGHT is a word the viewer translates, arriving at its different definitions.

This act of translating both mirrors and parallels what must be done with the warnings in French and German. Johns has placed the rectangle with OUGHT directly above the warnings. Likewise, the warning with its skull and crossbones is directly above the bathtub with its faucet and handles. Taken together these images can be read as a single bodiless figure consisting of a skull and genitals, a disembodied presence Johns previously explored in his *Tantric Detail* paintings.

The figure is distinctly male. Echoing this male figure is the *Mona Lisa* "poster," which has been placed directly above the George Ohr pot. The four-leafed, floral pattern visible in the pot mirrors the cruciform defining each of the faucet's two handles, thus suggesting that the figures of Mona Lisa and the skull and crossbones mirror each other. Between the faucet-genitals and the Ohr pot Johns has depicted a white porcelain vase, whose shape (positive space) defines the adjacent negative space as the profiles of a male (left side) and a female (right side). On the side closest to the alignment of the *Mona Lisa* and the Ohr pot is the profile of the male's face, while on the side closest to the alignment of the highway sign and the faucet is the female's profile. The opticality of the pot, which shifts between profiles and vase, underscores Johns's desire to keep his "united states" from disintegrating.

This optical image is a type of Rubin's figure.* Nearly two decades earlier Johns wrote, "The spy stations himself to observe the watchman." The profiles are both connected to and disconnected from the vase's body; they and the vase can't be seen simultaneously. In this context the figure 0 takes on another meaning; it embodies the moment when thinking, particularly along abstract lines, isolates one's mind from one's body. "I think, therefore I am," Descartes declared, as if his body was irrelevant. This is the "polar situation" Johns must avoid if he is to remain

---

* The Danish psychologist Edgar Rubin used optical images to discuss the relationship between the intelligence and observation.

true to his project. The *Mona Lisa* "poster," highway warning, and puzzle portrait are isolated from their own bodies. But the patterned door, Ohr pot, and faucet-genitals are also in the painting.

Because the cruciform ribs defining each handle are not in the same position, the viewer reads the one on the left as having been "turned" on. Johns has also depicted "water" (wax) flowing from the faucet. Since the left (or hot water) handle is rotated, we can read this image a number of ways. The male figure is pissing (a sign of the body's production of waste), and the bath is "on." Waste and cleanliness are intertwined. The image of liquid flowing from the faucet is located directly beneath rivulets of wax dripping down the wall. The warning "beware of falling ice" is directly above them. His body immersed in water, Johns knows the water (wax) is rising.

Whereas the warning on the left side is addressed to the public realm Johns inhabits, the warning on the right side is addressed to the private or artistic realm. Now that he has broken up the surface of his paintings into distinct images, he must be careful not to let them become too isolated from one another. At the same time, the visual rhyme linking the encaustic rivulets and the flowing water (the pissing figure) underscores Johns's desire to keep his practice connected to his body's journey through time. By collapsing and juxtaposing images (faucet-genitals and tub) and materials ("water" and encaustic), underscoring the differences and similarities connecting water and encaustic (both exist in either solid or liquid state), Johns has broken down the hierarchy between art making and daily life. Thus, the right side of the painting is Johns's assessment of the relationship both he and his materials have to reality. "The watchman 'serves' as a warning": Immersed in the tub, one sees the effects of time upon one's body. One can neither escape one's body nor preserve it.

Johns destroyed a flag in order to make a "flag." Then he destroyed it again in order to make another one. Each "flag" is unique even as it preserves the flag's basic design. Yet this ability to destroy something and then both resurrect and preserve it in its new form doesn't overcome the splits separating one's body and mind. Their coexistence is constantly in flux. No matter where the viewer finds entrance into *Racing Thoughts,* he or she will discern connections between one image and another, and between words and images, and between abstract patterning and a specific object. Once these connections are made, the viewer begins examining the multidirectional, multilayered readings that slowly make themselves apparent. Johns has constructed a dense web of coexisting narratives, which jostle for privilege. No story is more essential than any other.

For while the right side can be read as Johns's assessment of his relationship to both reality and art, it is also an homage to various artists who have influenced his private or artistic life. Johns alluded to Peto in the title, made explicit references to Newman, and, in the *Mona Lisa* "poster", evoked both Leonardo da Vinci and Marcel Duchamp. (In *L.H.O.O.Q.* [1919, Rechfied Readymade; pencil on reproduction, $7\ ^{3}/_{4}$ x $4\ ^{7}/_{8}$ in., private collection], Duchamp altered a reproduction of the *Mona Lisa* by adding a mustache and a goatee.) The pots underscore Johns's interest in George Ohr, a self-taught artist, and the nameless artisans who make things. None of these figures is given special attention. In this regard the left side is Johns's homage to Leo Castelli, who gave the artist his first show. Each object, rectangle, word, and mark in the painting has been put there for a reason. Through his attention to composition Johns has structured a perception in which everything is central. The rim of the tub calls attention to the fundamental subject of the painting, which is cleansing and change. These processes, the tub makes clear, cannot take place apart from the body.

Five

The Thinking Mind and the Animal Body

Between 1954 and 1983 Johns's subject matter consisted largely of preformed objects. After the two *Racing Thoughts* paintings (1983–84), he began expanding his vocabulary to include invented images. Among them are a trompe l'oeil blueprint of his grandparents' house, in which he spent part of his childhood, and a schematic face consisting of two eyeballs, each flush with a carefully delineated edge, a mouth that is also a mountain, and a curlicue that evokes the outline of someone's nostrils. Johns used these inventions to make direct allusions to his memories of childhood. Thus he has not only moved from one kind of painting to another, and expanded his vocabulary in an unlikely direction, but also changed his attitude toward disclosure. What enabled him to reinvent himself?

Since Johns has spent much of his career deliberately refusing to make any overt autobiographical references, the changes he made in the early 1980s must be regarded as significant. In *Racing Thoughts*, Johns began depicting images of various objects he owned, including the puzzle portrait, the Ohr pot, and the *Mona Lisa* poster. He placed these things in a room which alluded to the most private part of his house, the bathroom. However, the subject was the artist's life rather than personal memories. After all, memory, as Johns's *Flag* made clear, is not to be trusted; it interferes with one's experience of reality. So what changed in Johns's thinking that enabled him to reveal personal memories? And do these allusions connote some personal disclosure? Or do they embody another, larger meaning?

In *Untitled* (1984, oil on canvas, 75 x 50 in., private collection), Johns delineated a patterned, contoured ground that recalls the door in *Racing Thoughts,* and, as before, the composition of the interlocking pieces is based on the boil-covered demon in Grünewald's *Temptation of Saint Anthony* panel. Two trompe l'oeil images have been "taped" to the pink and green contoured ground. Both images are optical, and each has been "cut off" by the painting's side edges. On the left side, Johns has "taped" a white-bordered drawing, which depicts the black and green stripes of two optical flags stacked together. Looked at long enough this image provokes in the viewer an optical afterimage, in which the correctly colored stripes (red and white) will become visible when one looks at a white surface. Johns first investigated this optical image of the American flag in a painting, *Flags* (1965, oil on canvas with raised canvas, 72 x 48 in., collection of the artist), a number of drawings, and a print. This image embodies Johns's description: "When the spy irritates, we try to remove him."

On the right side, across from this optical reversal of the flag's stripes, Johns used an image based on a well-known drawing by W. E. Hill called "My Wife and My Mother-in-Law," first published in *Puck,* an English humor magazine, in 1915. Like the Rubin's figure in *Racing Thoughts,* the image is ambiguous. However, instead of shifting between figure and ground, it contains two radically different images, one of a young woman with a ribbon around her neck, the other of an old crone with an enormous nose and cleft chin. The young woman is looking away, while the old woman is turned toward the viewer. The turning head echoes the shift in attention the viewer has to make in order to see both images, as well as acknowledges time's effects on the body.

Each image in *Untitled* is self-contained yet cut off by either an edge of the painting or the layering of one image on top of another. Each image reformulates the relationship between figure and ground. The optical black and green stripes produce an afterimage. The wife/mother-in-law image must be recontextualized. Finally, the patterned, contoured ground defines both surface and form. The viewer cannot quite discern the form but recognizes that the contoured, rotating pattern hints at spatiality.

Two questions arise. What is "looking"? And what is "spying"? The spy, we should remember, "stations himself to observe the watchman," while "the watchman falls 'into' the 'trap' of looking." If we look at the painting but don't examine it, we are inclined to miss the afterimage produced by the green and black stripes and the optical shift between wife and mother-in-law. However, Johns has chosen images which compel us to see ourselves looking at the painting, denying us immediate visual satisfaction. We "spy" the images within images and recognize that one experience exists inside another. No experience is isolated from any other. What do all these distinct though linked visual experiences add up to?

Both the "taped" optical images take time to be seen; they remind us that looking and thinking must always work in tandem if understanding is to take place. At the same time both figures are connected to the painting's shifting ground, reminding us that thinking must be connected to the body.* The memories Johns visualized in a number of paintings which followed *Untitled* must be understood in this context. One's mind remembers, but one's body doesn't. How memory informs the body is not clear, and Johns doesn't pretend to be an expert on such matters. Memories are part of one's helpless behavior; they can come unbidden. Certainly the helpless aspect of Johns is very different now that he is in his 60's than it was when he was a young artist. One's past becomes longer

---

* Clearly, Johns has recontextualized the perceptual split he first investigated in *Racing Thoughts* (1983).

than one's future; it is an unavoidable consequence of growing older.

Can memory finally detach the thinker from his or her body, isolate that person from the world? It is a possibility that Johns addressed in *Racing Thoughts.* He has to ensure that any reference to the past is connected to the present. Even in remembering the mind's connection to the body must be acknowledged. Otherwise the paintings will seem nostalgic in their intent, and Johns excised this possibility from his work at the beginning of his career.

In *Untitled* (1988, encaustic on canvas, 38 x 26 in., private collection), Johns depicted a trompe l'oeil towel pinned to a wooden wall above a faucet, handles, and the edge of a bathtub. The towel contains Johns's reference to Picasso's disturbing painting *Straw Hat with Blue Leaf* (1936), in which the artist pushed the facial features to the perimeter. At the same time, Picasso collapsed a woman's head and torso together; the left eye caps a breastlike protuberance, the right eye is located on the side of another breastlike shape, and the toothless mouth can be read as the woman's vagina. That we can also read one protuberance as a nose and the other as a forehead makes the image akin to the wife/mother-in-law image Johns previously used. The woman's head/body is connected to a vase-like shape, which rests on a platform, suggesting that the entire image is really of a sculpture.

Given Johns's long interest in the mind/body relationship, as well as his use of a Rubin's figure, it is easy to see why Picasso's painting might have appealed to him.*

Both the towel and the Picasso are melting; the faucet below this image is "on," and water (wax) is running into the tub. Above the towel Johns has made a thick red horizontal brushstroke across the trompe l'oeil board; it too is dripping. The painting may have been inspired by the two Picasso anecdotes that Johns mentioned to me: Picasso's characterization of a painting by de Kooning as a "melted Picasso," and his childhood amazement that one doesn't melt like a sugar cube in the bathtub. However, knowing that Johns didn't simply respond to his dream, it seems unlikely that he was merely reprising these anecdotes here.

What was it about these anecdotes that engaged Johns's attention? Both of them have to do with dissolution. On the one hand, Johns is turning Picasso's dismissal of de Kooning back on its source; he has depicted a melting Picasso. On the other hand, it's as if Johns has reformulated his own painting *Weeping Women* (1975). And yet, because Picasso's head/torso is the center of Johns's

---

* Johns inserted Picasso's profile into a Rubin's figure in his lithograph *Cups 4 Picasso* (West Islip, U.L.A.E.: 1972, lithograph, printed in color, 14 1/8 x 32 1/4 in.).

attention, we must consider that this is what made his *Untitled* possible.

The mind may generate thoughts apart from the body, but the fates of mind and body are ultimately linked. The mind and body become one at the moment of ultimate dissolution; this is what the artist faces in *Untitled.* The site of the painting is the bath. Naked and alone, with the faucet "on," Johns knows that mortality is inescapable, that one's body and mind do "melt" together, that nothing is fixed or stable, not even the art one makes.

In *The Bath* (1988, encaustic on canvas, 48 1/4 x 60 1/4 in., Oeffentliche Kunstsammlung, Kunstmuseum, Basel), Johns made this potentially disturbing connection between mind and body more explicit by splitting Picasso's image into two unequal rectangles, one on either side of the faucet. Each image has been "taped" to a pale blue wall, which contains the spotted outline of the boil-covered demon. "The spy stations himself to observe the watchman," Johns wrote more than two decades ago, and, despite what this requires, he has remained true to his words. As in *Racing Thoughts, The Bath* mirrors the relationship between head and body when taking a bath. The split Picasso image underscores Johns's recognition that the body and the mind are separate but connected states.

In two recent paintings, *Montez Singing* (1989–90, oil

on canvas, 76 x 50 in., collection Douglas S. Cramer) and *Untitled* (1995, oil on canvas, 66 x 44 in., collection the artist), Johns makes explicit allusions to his childhood. Born in Augusta, Georgia, on May 15, 1930, Johns lived in South Carolina during his childhood and was raised partly by his paternal grandfather and his second wife, Montez, who used to play the piano and sing "Red Sails in the Sunset." In *Montez Singing* Johns has invented a schematic face which owes something to the woman in Picasso's *Straw Hat with Blue Leaf*; he has pushed the eyes and mouth to the edges of a vertical rectangle.

In the stenciled title, which runs along the bottom of the painting, Johns has combined his and his step-grandmother's name and the date: "M *J*O *J*N *O*T *H*E *N* Z *S*S *1*I *9*N *8*G *9*I *9*N *0*G" (italics mine). By alternating blue and red letters, he has distinguished between his name and date and the painting's title. Combined but separate, the words must be separated and recombined in order to be read. The viewer performs this operation in the mind's eye and reads, MONTEZ SINGING and JJOHNS198990. The title of the painting becomes a distinct visual experience within the composition.

Above the title Johns has depicted the rectangular, schematic face; the eyes are directed toward the center; they are looking inward. A trompe l'oeil towel has been "pinned" to the face. On the towel Johns has depicted the image of a sunset, a red sailboat, and waves. The source of these images is most likely the artist's imagination. Certainly the simple geometry of the sailboat suggests that the source was not a child's drawing.

Memory is part of one's life, but how is it part of one's body? We remember (see in the mind's eye) events, places, and objects that no longer exist, or if they do exist are utterly different than before. The image of the closed mouth–mountain suggests that such memories are part of one's essential landscape, that they occupy a place in one's existence. Yet what do these memories mean?

Johns's observation "the spy must remember and must remember himself and his remembering" distinguishes three kinds of memory. There is the act of remembering, which seems distinctly rooted in autobiography. There is the act of the mind remembering itself; one must never lose sight of the mind's capacity, even will, to disconnect itself from the body, and act in discord with the body. And there is the act of remembering memories, which is to say contextualizing this aspect of thinking. The "spy" must do all three.

The cartoony eyes looking in at the towel alert the viewer that Johns isn't merely recapitulating a memory of childhood; he is framing it. The frame consists of two eyes, nostrils, and a mouth; it is "spying" rather than "looking." Only by "spying" can Johns make his memory into art.

The "spying" implies a distance that can never be overcome, which Johns has made evident by distance between the eyes and the towel. The combination of words suggests that one aspect is part of another but that each is simultaneously distinct. Thus, the various aspects of one's being are both contingent upon and secluded from one another. How they bear upon and affect one another remains a mystery; and Johns, to his credit, doesn't presume to have the answer. Montez may sing through Johns, a reading which his combining of words suggests, but that doesn't mean that either he or we hear the song. And if the viewer does "hear" the song, it is because of the viewer's memories. Once again Johns has found a way to underscore the essential gap between all individuals.

In *Untitled* (1995) Johns has superimposed a black outline over a white one. The black outline is of the two knights from the Isenheim Altarpiece, and, based on his memory, the white outline is Johns's trompe l'oeil blueprint of his grandparents' house. Beneath both outlines, which have been collapsed together, the viewer sees the outer edges of another image, which bears a similarity to the boil-covered demon. The blueprint evokes a childhood memory; the knights are Johns's image of the "watchman" or body. What do memory and the body, past and present, have to do with each other? One looks at the world with one's animal faculties; both animals and human see. But remembering is a different form of seeing; it sees what isn't there. By collapsing these outlines together, Johns distinguishes between "looking" and "spying." At the same time, the falling figure evokes one's helpless passage through time, both backwards and forwards.

Untitled (1995) can be regarded as both a continuation and a reversal of *Flag* and other early works by Johns. In those works Johns "spied" something about reality in preformed, conventional items; he reexamined something he had looked at many times. The body (the act of seeing) could be said to have come first. However, starting with *Untitled* (1984), it is the mind (the act of thinking) which links disparate visual experiences; the mind structures the items in the painting. Whereas Johns once saw it and then painted it, now he paints it and then sees it.

In order to accomplish this reversal, Johns must use images, whether invented or found, which acknowledge the bond between mind and body as well as embody a distinct visual experience. This is what the elements of his new vocabulary have in common. Thus in *Untitled* (1995) the knights both fall toward the blueprint and are bonded to it; "the watchman leaves his job & takes away no information." Whatever the body endured, it is the mind that does the remembering. The past is always remote and the future is always hurrying toward us. Yet, as in *Flag*, Johns layers his composition as the primary way of structuring his perception of flux. We see first one outline and then the other; memory and the body are distinct entities which are bound together.

After Holbein (1993, encaustic on canvas, 39 9/16 x 25 5/8 in., collection the artist) is based on Hans Holbein the Younger's watercolor-drawing *Portrait of a Young Nobleman Holding a Lemur* (c. 1541–42, pen, ink, and watercolor on paper, Oeffentliche Kunstsammlung, Kunstmuseum, Basel). Holbein did the portrait shortly before his sudden death from the plague in London in 1543. He was around age forty-six.

Holbein's faded, damaged watercolor has a flat blue background against which the young nobleman is posed frontally, cradling a lemur in his arms. The nobleman is either standing or seated in front of a table, on which his right arm seems to be resting. He looks to be in his adolescence, and is dressed in a plumed hat and bulky clothes. The combination of the watercolor's layered pictorial space with the silhouette of the face may have been the formal reason it appealed to Johns.*

As in Johns's paintings Holbein's approach is clinical and non-hierarchical. Concerned with exactitude rather

---

* In a conversation with the author, Johns mentioned that he owned three marmosets in the mid-1960s (the marmoset is related to the lemur).

than flattery, Holbein paid the same attention to the prince, his regal attire, and the monkey. Because the watercolor was exposed to sunlight, many of the features are faded, leaving ghostly outlines. Thus the blue background is more evident than the man's face, which is now but a few pencil lines. There are also two sections missing. One tear is at the top, near the center, and the other is on the right side, near the prince's shoulder. Johns has taken all these aspects into account.

Johns has combined a contour line with two patterns: wood grain, and rows of ascending sperm. The layered space doesn't thrust forward, as it did when Johns "taped" the *Mona Lisa* poster to the wall; it is receding into the painting's ground; separated only by the contour lines, the prince's wood-grain face is becoming part of the wood-grain wall. One thing is becoming another. It's as if Johns is looking toward the future, the moment when the last traces of the prince's ghostly face have faded forever, leaving only a blank sheet of paper.* Using Johns's vocabulary, it can be said that because of the sun the original ground (or white paper) has started "eating" the man's face.

---

* Johns once told me of a Magritte drawing he owned and the fact that the drawing had faded. He took it to a conservator, who told him that nothing could be done; the drawing had faded completely and there was nothing left to conserve. The issue then is, What do you do with this blank sheet of paper?

Whereas Holbein drew a portrait of a specific individual, which has since faded into a silhouette, Johns has used a contour line and patterning to suppress all traces of the individual's physiognomy. It is not the faded traces of the individual's outward look but the silhouette of a young man holding a lemur that he wanted to transfer from the Holbein drawing to his own work. In Holbein's portrait Johns encountered an image which mirrors his interest in the separate but linked states constituting the individual's existence. The nobleman is another example of Johns's "watchman." He can leave his job and take away no information because the body is unable to reflect upon its own existence. The mind (nobleman) and body (lemur) are distinct but linked entities.

In *Perilous Night* the exterior and interior of the outlined figure are black. In *After Holbein* the relationship of figure and ground is more complex, though no less direct. Both figure and ground are defined by either trompe l'oeil wood grain or rows of ascending sperm. The gray encaustic is semitransparent in areas, the wood grain starting to show through. In other areas the encaustic has started to melt, and the sperm become a drip of dark paint mixing with the gray. Again, using Johns's vocabulary, the figure and ground have both "eaten" and "been eaten" by each other; it is this moment of entanglement, and all that it implies, that Johns has preserved in encaustic.

There is something haunting about Johns's outline of a face and hands filled in with wood grain. The shape of the face, the plumed hat, and the large, round shoulders evoke a young, robust man. Yet he is faceless and thus remains nameless in a deep, essential way. Who among us hasn't heard of someone who vanished, before he achieved his potential? *After Holbein* provokes these recognitions without pointing directly to an individual. We don't even need to know the identity of the young man. Johns's painting isn't about death, premature or otherwise, in some anecdotal way. It doesn't privilege one death or kind of death over another. The frontality of Johns's depictions underscores his intention to keep his eyes open, to keep looking at the world from which and into which he is passing.

For all the isolation that informed Johns's early work, and the intensity of knowing that this state was finally inescapable, Johns recognizes that eventually he will become part of the world, that this is the destiny we all share. Unlike many of his contemporaries, Johns makes no attempt to hide his fate. The difference between his early paintings and his recent ones is not purely formal. Rather the isolation he embodied in his early work was of the kind we associate with being a young man; it was seclusion from the world. The pictorial space in Johns's recent paintings conveys a sea change in his thinking; the rooms filled with objects underscore his acknowledgment of being part of something far larger than the individual; the seclusion takes place in a world.

Johns's "rooms" are no more straightforward than his "flags." The faucet is "on"; life is continually draining away, even as we renew ourselves. The "wooden" ground of *After Holbein* is the "ground" toward which time is bearing us, even now. And while we might wish to read the "wood" as coffin, that conclusion is too reductive. For Johns knows that life (the rows of rising sperm) goes on without us, that it doesn't need any one of us any more than any other.

For all that we have repeatedly told Johns about his genius and importance to art history, what is compelling now is that he has never let that become a guiding principle in his art, has never allowed our praise to become a refuge. *After Holbein* isn't about Johns but about whoever views it. That Johns can be both so matter-of-fact and so thoughtful about what is particular, as well as common, to being alive in this world is the riveting thing about the painting. The directness with which he looks at reality and recognizes himself in it is finally the only measure we should apply to him and his work. What we should recognize now is that it isn't genius so much as humility and courage that Johns brings to bear his art. Such a measure could prove eminently useful, particularly if we should try to live up to it. More than forty years ago, Johns had a dream. He showed us what the dream showed him. Perhaps it is time we take its lesson to heart.

Notes

The Jasper Johns epigraph is from David Sylvester, "Interview," in *Jasper Johns: Drawings* (catalog of an exhibition organized by the Arts Council of Great Britain, 1974), p. 7.

1 David Sylvester, "Interview," in *Jasper Johns: Drawings* (catalogue of an exhibition organized by the Arts Council of Great Britain, 1974), p. 7.

2 Conversation with the author.

3 David Sylvester and Sarah Whitfield, *René Magritte: Catalogue Raisonné. Volume 1: Oil Paintings, 1916–1930* (Antwerp: Menil Foundation and Electa/Fonds/Mercator, 1992), pp. 239–40.

4 See also David Sylvester and Sarah Whitfield, *René Magritte: Catalogue Raisonné. Volume 2: Oil Paintings and Objects, 1931–1948* (Antwerp: Menil Foundation and Electa/Fonds/Mercator, 1993), p. 199.

5 Sylvester and Whitfield, *René Magritte,* Vol. 1, pp. 239–40.

6 Michael Crichton, *Jasper Johns* (New York: Abrams, in association with the Whitney Museum of American Art, 1977), p. 27.

7 Jasper Johns, "Sketchbook Notes, " *Art and Literature 4* (Lausanne, Switzerland: Spring 1965), pp. 191–192; reprinted in John Russell and Suzi Gablik, *Pop Art Redefined* (New York: Praeger, 1969) pp. 84–85; reprinted in Kristine Stiles and Peter Selz, *Theories and Documents of Contemporary Art: A Sourcebook of Artists' Writings* (Berkeley: University of California Press, 1996) pp. 325–326. Johns also published two other selections of "Sketchbook Notes." One appeared in *Juillard*, edited and published by Trevor Winkfield (Leeds, England, Winter 1968–69), pp. 25–27, the other in *Art Now: New York*, (vol. 1, no. 4, April 1969).

8 Reprinted in Robert Lebel, *Marcel Duchamp,* trans. George Heard Hamilton (New York: Grove Press, 1959), pp. 77–78.

9 Conversation with the author.

10 Ibid.

11 Thomas B. Hess, *Barnett Newman* (New York: Museum of Modern Art, 1973), pp. 94–107.

List of Plates

cover: *After Holbein,* 1993, encaustic on canvas, 48 1/8 x 75 1/8 in.
Collection the artist.
Photograph by Dorothy Zeidman.

Flag, 1955, encaustic and collage on canvas, 41 1/4 x 60 3/4 in. The Museum of Modern Art, New York.
Gift of Philip Johnson in honor of Alfred Barr.
Photograph by Rudolph Burckhardt.

Map, 1963, encaustic and collage on canvas, 60 x 93 in.
Private collection, New York.
Photograph by Rudolph Burckhardt.

Between the Clock and the Bed, 1982–3, encaustic on canvas (three panels), 72 x 126 1/8 in.
Sydney and Frances Lewis Foundation, Richmond, Virginia.
Photograph by Dorothy Zeidman.

Perilous Night, 1982, encaustic on canvas with objects, 67 x 96 x 5 in.
Collection Robert and Jane Meyerhoff, Phoenix, Maryland.
Photograph by Glenn Steigelman.

Tantric Detail I, 1980, oil on canvas, 50 1/8 x 34 1/8 in.
Collection the artist.
Photograph by Jim Strong.

Racing Thoughts, 1983, encaustic and collage on canvas, 48 1/8 x 75 1/8 in.
The Whitney Museum of American Art. Purchased with funds from the Burroughs Wellcome Purchase Fund; Leo Castelli; the Wilfred P. and Rose J. Cohen Purchase Fund; the Julia B. Engel Purchase Fund; the Equitable Life Assurance Society of the United States Purchase Fund; the Sondra and Charles Gilman, Jr. Foundation, Inc.; S. Sidney Kahan; The Lauder Foundation, Leonard and Evelyn Lauder Fund; the Sara Roby Foundation; and the Painting and Sculpture Committee. 84.6.
Photograph by Dorothy Zeidman.

Untitled, 1984, oil on canvas, 75 x 50 in.
Private collection.
Photograph by Dorothy Zeidman.

Untitled, 1988, encaustic on canvas, 38 x 26.
Private collection.
Photograph by Dorothy Zeidman.

Montez Singing, 1989, oil on canvas, 76 x 50 in.
Collection Douglas S. Cramer.
Photograph by Dorothy Zeidman.

Untitled, 1995, oil on canvas, 66 x 44 in.
Collection the artist.
Photograph by Dorothy Zeidman.